"In *Illegal* John Denne... most pressing matters ... of the United States? ...pp...s to an idealistic young American abroad? Borders, national identity, justice. And then love, cutting through it all. How do two young lovers hold on to each other in the maelstrom of national politics and the swings of history? As Dennehy throws himself into the political and social life of Ecuador, you will see some of yourself in him."
—Cullen Thomas, author of *Brother One Cell*

"John Dennehy's memoir of love, life and illegally crossing borders in beautiful, but tumultuous Ecuador is told with vulnerability, honesty and is absolutely riveting. *Illegal* made me feel like I was hidden in the pages of Dennehy's passport—unsure what was going to happen next, longing for a life that may have disappeared, and never wanting the adventure to end."
—Katie McKenna, author of *How to Get Run Over by a Truck*

"Powerful and relatable. The pages resonated with me in a way I can't quite quantify. Beautiful to see someone put themselves out there like this."
—Zac Thompson, author of *Weaponized*

"Compellingly written, Dennehy's memoir of a tumultuous time of love and danger promises to be an exciting read with an ending that might land somewhere on the dark side of happy. Unlike so many journalists who can't leave the just-the-facts-ma'am style behind when they attempt book length manuscripts, Dennehy writes like a master storyteller."
—S.T. Ranscht, co-author of *Enhanced*

Illegal

John Dennehy grew up in New York but left the country when George Bush was reelected. For six years he lived in the developing world before returning to New York where he works for the United Nations. He has an MA in Creative Nonfiction from the University of East Anglia (England) and is frequently published in places such as VICE, The Guardian, Narratively and The Diplomat. This is his first book.

Illegal is the Gold medal winner of the Wishing Shelf awards, was named a Notable Indie by Shelf Unbound and won the Di Vinci Eye in the Eric Hoffer awards, among other awards and honors.

Illegal

A true story of love, revolution
and crossing borders

COTOPAXI
PUBLISHING

Second edition. Cotopaxi Publishing.

New York City

ISBN   978-0-9991852-3-0
eISBN: 978-0-9991852-1-6

For my parents

Everything in these pages is true, although some names and identifying details have been changed to provide anonymity to other characters in the story. The dialogues have been reconstructed from memory and journal notes. With rare exceptions, conversations and mutterings that took place in Spanish have been translated into English.

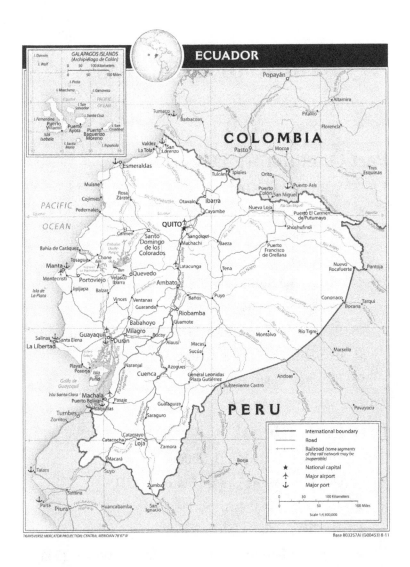

ECUADOR

Table of Contents

❖ October 3, 2006 (12)

Part One: Before Deportation

❖ Without Me (18)

❖ My First Revolution (29)

❖ In the Shadow of a Volcano (48)

❖ *Mi Amor* (65)

❖ Where the Sun Rises (76)

❖ In Motion (83)

❖ Behind the Barricades: Love and Revolution (90)

❖ Crossing the Border with Lucía (105)

❖ Bleeding Hearts (121)

Part Two: Illegal

Crossing One: October 3, 2006

❖ Deported to the United States (131)

❖ A Prisoner in the Airport (135)

❖ The Boy with the Flower (139)

❖ Running Barefoot at Houston International (144)

❖ Colombia (151)

❖ No, Officer, I Don't Have Any Cocaine (154)

Crossing Two: November 17, 2006

❖ Home, again   (158)

❖ Just Another Gringo in Colombia   (164)

❖ Losing My Way   (170)

❖ Lying to the Police   (173)

Crossing Three: January 25, 2007

❖ The Agony of Borders (184)

Crossing Four: March 29, 2007

❖ Giving Up on Hope   (202)

❖ The Help of Strangers   (208)

Crossing Five: April 23, 2007

❖ The Final Crossing   (217)

Epilogue

❖ Ecuador, 2017   (222)

October 3, 2006

Two policemen grab me by the shoulders and pull me away from the immigration counter at Quito International Airport.

"*¿Qué hice?*" I ask, my voice shaking.

I try to see their faces but the police turn from me. Each one jabs an arm in the space between my arm and torso, curls an elbow under my armpit, and locks a hand on my shoulder. Facing the opposite direction from me, they march forward, pushing my upper body with them and forcing my feet to backpedal. A third officer walks in front, leading us against the flow of passengers moving toward passport control.

"*¿Qué hice?*" I ask louder.

Silence.

"*¿Qué hice?!*"

The other travelers stare but the police keep dragging me. I turn my head and see a half-dozen more officers standing under the staircase in the corner of the massive room, keeping an eye on us as we approach.

When we reach the larger group the two policemen holding me relax their grips. The one on my right takes a step back to face me. He's young, about my age, and his crisp, olive green hat is too small for his head. He looks down to avoid my eyes and tells me, "*Usted estará en nuestra custodia hasta que…*—You will be in our custody until you are flown back to the United States. I can't tell you anything else." He pauses and lifts his head, though his eyes still avoid mine. "I'm sorry."

I know his conscience can be a weakness. A mix of Ecuadorian families pushing over-packed luggage and Western tourists with expensive, steel-framed backpacks are streaming by us. They are walking down the stairs above us and continuing toward the immigration lines. Most pass without seeing us, but I know I can draw their attention. And I know the police don't want a scene. It's my only leverage.

"*Necesito ver a mi novia*—I need to see my girlfriend." The words rush out. "She's waiting for me and won't know what happened."

I had seen her on my way in, standing behind the pane of glass that separated a small food court from the long hallway toward immigration control. She was holding a sunflower and waving; smiling; waiting. She will have seen everyone from my flight pass through by now, and I wonder if she is already piecing things together. She still has a copy of my passport and instructions for whom to call if I'm arrested—souvenirs from our trouble at the Colombian border a month before when the overweight officer in Ecuador threatened me with five years in jail if I tried to sneak in.

My mind flashes between her two faces: one waving at me from behind the glass, smiling and excited; another sitting at arrivals, biting her lip like she does before she cries.

Six months before, when *la Revolución Ciudadana*—the Citizens' Revolution—began and all the highways were blockaded, she came for me. I had spent the day at a seized bridge downtown, talking with the rebels and trying to understand why they were willing to risk so much to prevent a free-trade agreement with the United States. All the schools and businesses were closed either out of solidarity or fear and Lucía spent the day hitchhiking through the rebels' barricades so we could be together during the chaos. I already knew parts of her complicated past by then; a month before she had started to reveal to me the various layers of her broken marriage. When we collapsed onto my bed that night, still coughing from the tear gas lingering over the city, I decided that if we could be together that day then we would on every day to come.

"I need to see my girlfriend," I say again, to no one in particular, scanning the faces of the police. The passengers waiting in line had stared when the uniformed men pushed me across the room, but now their attention has moved on. I can see people thumbing through passports, inching forward, oblivious.

"I need to see my girlfriend," I say yet again, louder; loud enough for others to hear. I'm on the verge of screaming and can feel myself beginning to tremble. "I live here. I work here. And I need to see my girlfriend!"

Passengers walking past slow down and look on curiously. The police are not holding me anymore, but they form a perimeter around my body. When I shout again they all take a step in, tightening the circle. I can smell their cologne and sweat above the sterile monotony of airport disinfectant. Passengers stop and stare. Some already in line look back.

"I didn't do anything wrong! Please, I need to see my girlfriend."

My mind races back to the argument we'd had the night before my trip, to the insults we threw at each other. It makes me that much more desperate to see her, to tell her that I still love her, that I will always love her.

A lot of passengers are watching. I lower my voice and stare at the officer in front of me, the one who led the two policemen from the counter. His dark brown eyes meet mine and stare back. He blinks and I can see tiny wrinkles branch out in fine lines as his eyelids shut.

"What's her name?" he asks.

"Lucía. She has black hair, black jeans and is wearing a white

T-shirt with hearts. She's holding a sunflower."

"I'll look for her," he says.

I sit down on the cold, tiled floor and the remaining police relax. The passengers move on.

For the first time in my life I know exactly where I want to be. I have found my home in the shadow of an Andean volcano in Ecuador. I'm about to move in with the woman that I love, and I'm directly involved with a revolution that's not just changing my adoptive nation but changing me. Now all of this is in peril.

How will I find another professor to cover my classes at the university? How can I get rent money to my landlord? A thousand prosaic, practical details rush through my brain but my thoughts always return to her, to Lucía.

I jump to my feet when I see her. I want to run to her but the uniforms close their circle around me again. I stand still and watch her walk toward me. Her eyes are red and she wipes away the tears when she gets close.

The police open the circle, allowing her to pass, then close it again, trapping us both inside. She puts her arms around me, creating a bubble. Nothing else is real, nothing else matters.

We are silent. My hands slide down her body and rest on the small of her back. My fingers pull on her shirt, bunching it into a ball inside my fist. We instinctively move our bodies up against each other; our legs intertwine and her breasts press against me. Our faces touch and I feel her warm skin against mine, our tears mixing on each other's cheeks. I close my eyes and inhale, smelling her, remembering the taste of her neck. We lift our heads and touch our lips, opening, tasting each other's salt. When we return our heads to each other's shoulders we let the water run.

The image of Lucía and the thought of seeing her had kept me focused and held me together. Now that she is in my arms I let go.

The tears don't streak into droplets; they flow down my cheek in a steady stream. Our mouths, next to each other's ears, whisper "*te amo*" over and over again.

I know the police will soon separate us. I know that everything will change. I know that I am losing all that I had. I feel helpless and overwhelmed, as if drowning in slow motion.

In her ear I whisper, "*Voy a volar a Colombia y cruzar la frontera clandestinamente*— I will fly to Colombia and sneak across the border. Nothing else matters. I love you."

Lucía steps back and pulls a camera from her bag. The movement, the loss of her body against mine, jolts me back into reality. The police are staring at us, peering into what had seemed such a private and intimate place just seconds before. Lucía hands one of our guards the camera and, for some strange reason, has him take a picture of us, freezing that moment in time.

In the photo we have our arms around each other, our eyes, red from sobbing, are looking right into the lens.

I had wiped away the tears before looking into the camera, but deep down, deeper than I would comprehend for months to come, there was no pretending.

"We have to move," the officer with the dark brown eyes says. The same two police grab my shoulders and pull me away.

Thirty days before I meet the president; eight weeks before Lucía tells me her husband has put a price on my head and hired a hit man; three months before I walk away from the barricades and decide to fight against the revolution rather than for it; half a year before I give up—I am deported.

BEFORE

Without Me

It was a few hours after sunset when the plane touched down at Quito International Airport. There was no line at immigration and I walked right through. This was March 2005 and nearly two years before I was deported. I was twenty-two years old and holding a mostly empty passport—I had left the United States for the first time less than a year ago, while still in university.

Outside the terminal, taxis waited by the curb. They were yellow, just like New York. I hadn't checked a bag and was the first one through from my flight. Drivers were shouting questions at me—I assumed they were asking where I wanted to go. A few ran up to greet me while they spat out streams of sounds. I took out my notebook and read a phrase I had copied from the Spanish/ English dictionary on the plane ride down, "*Un hotel barato y cerca el terminal de buses por favor*—A cheap hotel near the bus station please."

A man with grey stubble and a too-big sweater grabbed my bag from me and opened the front door of his taxi. He smelled like diesel.

As we pulled off the curb I understood his first question and told him, "*Yo soy de Nueva York.*"

He nodded and followed up with another question, his brown eyes glancing at me, waiting for an answer.

I shrugged my shoulders. "I don't speak Spanish."

He smiled and said something else in his language.

We were each having our own conversation.

Once we got away from the airport the city was quiet. At first things seemed fairly modern; there were two and three story blocks of concrete made into apartments with occasional storefronts at street level. There were billboards hanging above the street, illuminated with spotlights. The road changed from smooth pavement to cobblestone. It began to look more urban, though the streets stayed empty. Storefronts were covered in sheets of metal pulled down and locked into hooks poking up from the sidewalk. A blue glow sneaked around closed curtains of a few windows but many were just dark.

There were now traffic lights at most intersections. We sped through green and red just the same—though the driver would sound his horn a few times when we approached red ones. The buildings became taller and narrower, pushing up against each other. We swerved round a concrete pole in the road. Ahead was a whole line of them, as far as the eye could see. Most of them grew out of the sidewalk but a few sprouted from the cobblestone street, forcing cars to swerve around them. A nest of wires stood atop each one, branching out in every direction.

The driver stopped at a green light and beeped his horn. There was a round woman sitting on a stool next to a wooden cart lit by a burning candle. He shouted something out the window to her and she jumped to her feet, grabbed something off her cart and rushed over to us. Her cheeks were almost red, though her skin was fairly dark. She wore a black felt hat with what seemed to be a peacock feather sticking out of it. I saw she had a blanket tied across her chest but only when she reached the window did I see there was a baby snuggled inside, hanging off her back. She handed over a pack of gum to the driver just as the light turned red. He opened the pack, turned toward me and reached his hand out.

"*Gracias*," I said as he tilted the box and let a piece fall onto my open palm.

The next morning I walked across the street from my hotel and boarded a bus to Cuenca, a city eight hours south along winding roads that moved down the spine of the Andes.

I followed our progress across Ecuador on my map. Each time we stopped at a new town I found its little black dot and watched as we crept away from Quito and toward Cuenca. When the bus entered Cuenca I pressed my face to the window and stared out onto my new home.

*

The week that the Iraq War began in 2003 was also my Spring Break. I left my university in Hartford and went back to New York for a few days. On St. Patrick's Day I joined a few friends and we took the train into Manhattan to see the parade. I knew there would be a lot of people out in the streets so I spray painted "No War On Iraq" across the front of an old T-shirt. I thought it'd be a passive way to get the message into people's heads. Lots of other people, drunk at a parade and primed for war by months of build-up, saw it as provocative. All day people caught my eye and gave me dirty looks. A few shouted things such as "Communist!" and "Get out of the country!"

As the parade began to wind down I was standing on a side street, half a block away from the crowd on 5th Ave. My friend and I were waiting for a few other friends who had gone off to get food. A group of high school kids, about 16 or 17 years old, stopped in front of me.

"Why are you wearing that shirt?" asked one boy.

"Because there's no reason for war."

"What about 9/11? You think we should just not do anything?" His fists were clenched at his sides. Twelve of his friends stood behind him, crowding around, excited for some action. His arms were almost hairless. His face was pockmarked with pimples.

"9/11 was horrible but had nothing to do with Iraq. The problem is—"

Warm saliva splashed across my face. I reflexively wiped my hand across my cheek.

From the cluster behind the pimpled boy somebody yelled. "Hit 'im. He's a fucking traitor!"

My friend jumped in front, trying to defend me, and took the first punch square in the jaw. They swarmed around us, knocked us to the ground and kicked us in the face and chest. My friend got up, connected a few punches and ended up on the ground again, sneakers smacking against him. I curled up in a ball and covered my face with my forearms. A dozen skinny legs wound up and kicked against the back of my head and my chest. Everything moved in slow motion. I watched the kicks connect but didn't feel or hear anything. I felt empty. There was no impulse to grab one of them and fight back.

When they stopped and ran off I looked up and saw a crowd of spectators around us. A hundred people had watched and let it play out. My friend was worse off than me. Both his eyes were already swelling, and one of them was filled with blood.

Two days later the U.S. military started bombing Baghdad and invaded Iraq.

I sat down with my parents at the kitchen table and told them what I planned to do. Over the past year I had become quickly immersed in activism at the University of Hartford, where I was in my junior year of college. I was president of a newly resurgent Progressive Student Alliance which had become the largest student organization on campus. I sent my parents clippings from newspaper articles and told them about the various protests and teach-ins we organized. I think they knew what was coming;

for weeks news stories had circulated that groups were planning massive civil disobedience if the war started.

"On Monday morning a group of us are going to block the doors to the Federal building in Hartford."

"And then what?" my father asked. He was a business manager and always calculated everything in advance. "What happens when the police come?"

"We stay. The goal is to stop the government from working that day, at least at that one building."

My mom, who was a teacher and volunteered at a homeless shelter, leaned forward in her chair. "They'll arrest you," she said. "You can keep going to protests and writing letters and all of that but if you get arrested it will stay with you. It will go on your permanent record."

"I want this on my permanent record."

On Monday we locked arms and blocked all the entrances before anyone arrived. "Government's closed until the war's over," we told the employees as they arrived. The police came and dragged us away. I let my body go limp and four officers in riot gear carried me onto a waiting bus. It felt good to so forcefully declare opposition to what was being done in my name.

But it also felt pathetic. Bombs were falling on cities and the best I could do was block a door.

That night Hartford police officers brought a boom box down to the holding cells, now filled with anti-war protesters. They played the "Star-Spangled Banner" on repeat through the night.

That's the night my faith began to crack. I kept going to protests. I kept writing letters and signing petitions. And I kept urging people to vote for good, progressive candidates.

But I didn't believe it anymore.

When I dived into activism I thought we would win. I thought you could follow all the rules, and if you worked hard enough, you would win. All you had to do was work hard, every day, and government would listen, and society would change. Aided by the naiveté of youth, I thought I could change the world ... until I didn't.

The morning after my arrest, I was given a court date and released. There were a dozen supporters waiting outside and a few friends from university who drove me back and dropped me off at my dorm. My roommate was at class and I closed the door behind me. I didn't want to wash off the dirt of a night in the cells just yet. I wrote poetry instead.

my country is going to war; without me
my nation is planning to kill; without me
my president has abandoned peace; without me

After the Iraq War started George W. Bush began referring to himself as a 'war president.' When he was re-elected a few months later I decided to leave the country. I was in my final semester at the University of Hartford and the timing was right; I just needed a place to go. I had read about workers taking over factories in Argentina and Hugo Chavez winning elections in Venezuela but not much else about South America. There was almost no one paying attention to the continent, except for this vague notion that American style capitalism was being challenged there, and that drew me toward it. I wanted to find something that stood in contrast to America, and I also liked the idea of a fresh slate that I would mostly color with firsthand experience rather than preconceived notions. Cuenca, Ecuador was simply the place where I found a job from an online posting.

When I arrived at the Cuenca bus station for the first time in March 2005, there was a large plaque honoring the city's recent designation as a UNESCO World Heritage Site. I had the address of the school that had hired me and it was close enough to walk. I had only a single duffel bag with a few changes of clothes so I didn't mind exploring a bit on my way. The city was full of narrow cobblestone streets and they were crowded with people. The first thing that struck me were the colors. In the late afternoon sun every building seemed to be painted a different shade. Bright oranges and greens and blues were framed by the red clay-tile roofs that hung over most buildings. Even window frames and shutters were painted purple or magenta or some other wild color that stood in contrast to the wall around it.

There were a lot of round women with rosy cheeks like the one I had seen in Quito. Some also carried babies in the same style, tucked in a blanket behind their backs. All of them wore long skirts that hung down to their ankles. Mixed within the crowds were a lot of foreigners. Some were wearing big backpacks and studying maps at corners while others walked confidently down side streets and into houses. I heard some of them speaking English and when I got lost, I asked one group for directions. "Do you work there?" asked a man with a mid-western accent.

"Yeah, starting next week."

"Sweet. I have some friends working there too." I was close and he gave me directions to get me to the front door.

"Thanks."

"No problem. I'm sure I'll be seeing you around. Welcome to Cuenca."

At my new school I met the director, Fiona. She was from Ireland and had come to the school to teach two years before, and had quickly moved up the ranks. Her office was sparsely decorated, and the walls were freshly painted a bright lime-green. We sat across from each other in plush office chairs, her desk between us filled with workbooks and lesson plans.

"*Eres gato también*," she said.

"What?"

"Oh sorry, sometimes I forget which language I'm supposed to use." She smiled. Her green eyes blinked and made contact with mine. "I was just noticing your light blue eyes. Almost all Ecuadorians have brown eyes so green or blue is a novelty here. Everyone will call you *gato* when they meet you. It means cat. It can become annoying but it's definitely a compliment; everyone wants to be *gato* here."

After our casual introductions, she asked me a simple question that would have far-reaching consequences over the next years of my life: Did I want the school to get me a work visa?

"That's optional?" I asked, confused.

She laughed. "Well, most foreigners who work in Ecuador come with governments or large international organizations, like the Peace Corps or WorldTeach, and work visas are part of the program. Not many people come here independently, and the ones who do usually just renew their automatic tourist visa every ninety days."

"Oh, and how can I renew my tourist visa?"

"All you have to do is leave the country and come back. There are some nice beaches a few hours away in Peru that a lot of people go to. Of course we could get you a work visa and then you won't have to worry about it. You just need to give me your passport and $180 and the school will take care of everything."

"Can I think about it?"

"Sure. Just let me know before the first week of classes finish." She paused and then asked, "Have you seen the library yet?" She smiled, and though it was our first meeting, she seemed more like an old friend. Our minority status in what was a very different world from 'home' provided an instant bond. "You may take out as many books as you want; it's one of the perks of working here," she said as she stood up to lead me downstairs.

I checked out *Walden* and *Civil Disobedience* by Henry David Thoreau and left the school. It was warm and sunny. A few blocks away I stumbled upon a school with a small plaza at its entrance. I sat down on a bench, the sidewalk and street in front of me and behind me a low concrete wall that held soil and a small garden. I had already read Thoreau in a literature class at university but wanted to read him in a different context. I wanted to let his ideas flow through me as I set out on a new beginning.

Fiona made the visa decision sound unimportant, and I believed it would be. But I was still high on symbolism and the idea that I could do things differently—I was bitter about having followed all the rules in the U.S. but having it amount to nothing. Perhaps the choice would only be symbolic, but I resolved to begin my new life outside the United States by living as I thought things should be, rather than how they were.

Before I moved to Ecuador I'd never had to think about borders very much. I would have said I didn't like them but it would have been based on vague emotion more than reality. That wasn't good enough. I wanted to break down the logic of national borders and decide what I thought would fit best into my hypothetical ideal.

Borders are lines between nations, deciding where one government's power begins and another ends. They are barriers designed to control the flow of information, commerce, goods, services and people. In theory, a border will keep out the bad while allowing the good to pass through, something akin to how a window screen will let in fresh air but not mosquitoes. A great theory, but the more I thought about the reality of the border, the less I liked it.

In modern times barriers to commerce have come down significantly, if not entirely, to allow for easier trade. The world has never been smaller or more connected, so rather than acting as barriers, borders have become little more than ports of entry—unless you're human. With the rise of globalization, goods and services have gained greater freedom of movement and humans have lost it. Sneakers can travel anywhere in the world to be sold, but the person who made them cannot follow.

I went to a bookstore Fiona had told me about and scoured the shelves for information to back up my gut feelings about borders. I bought a used copy of *Opening the Floodgates: Why America Needs to Rethink its Borders and Immigration Laws* by Kevin Johnson and I covered the margins with notes.

Johnson says that migration flows are hindered mostly by culture, language or distance rather than strict border restrictions. People tend to stay in their own comfort zones except in cases of extreme inequality or threat of violence, and in those cases fences don't do much good anyway.

That was the intellectual argument, but there was also an emotional one. Why should I be able to travel to Ecuador because I was born in the U.S. while an Ecuadorian could not travel to the U.S. because he was born in Ecuador? Borders seemed designed to help keep transnational economic power dynamics stagnant, to entrench inequality.

I also read and reread *Civil Disobedience*, and let Thoreau's message guide me: "Let your life be a friction to stop the machine." The institutions of power pull their force from the individuals who submit to them, and participation in them, even in opposition, strengthens them, lends credibility and can actually be one of the biggest obstacles to fundamental change. Therefore, abstaining from the system completely, depriving it of your power is the true revolutionary act. "[The state] can have no pure right over my person and property but what I concede to it."

I decided to forgo the work visa. I was choosing not to participate in a global system that made vastly different rules for world citizens based solely on place of birth. There was a fair bit of irony in that I was only in a position to make that choice because of that same privilege; only because of my U.S. citizenship could I travel freely between Ecuador and her neighbors to automatically renew my visa.

At the time it seemed that it wouldn't matter much either way, so I made what I thought was a mostly symbolic choice to never ask permission.

My First Revolution

Political demonstrations occur frequently throughout Ecuador for various reasons. Protesters often block city streets and rural highways, including major arteries such as the Pan American Highway. Public transportation is often disrupted during these events. Protesters may burn tires, throw rocks and Molotov cocktails, engage in destruction of property and detonate small improvised explosive devices during demonstrations. Police response may include water cannons and tear gas. United States citizens are advised to avoid areas where demonstrations are in progress.

–Excerpt from U.S. Department of State Profile of Ecuador (2006)

When I arrived in Ecuador there was already a political conflict brewing. It was splashed across the front pages of the newspapers and echoed in conversations throughout the country. But I didn't speak Spanish, so it took me a while to catch on.

I started teaching right away.

"I suppose I'll have a more advanced group, since my Spanish is so poor," I said to Fiona.

"No. Actually you'll be with children six to eleven years old. But don't worry, we have a policy that no one can speak Spanish inside the classroom, and that includes teachers."

I must have looked unconvinced.

"You'll be fine. I'll show you the lesson plans; just follow those and you'll be fine. And everyone has been in your position before. I'm sure the other teachers who stayed over from last term will be very helpful."

The main campus was a new three story brick building on the edge of downtown. The classrooms all had new desks and whiteboards, while the teachers' lounge had comfortable chairs and even a few couches. It was not very different from schools I had been in back in the United States, except classroom sizes tended to be smaller and all the students wore uniforms. This school didn't require a uniform but most students came straight from their classes in the public school which did. Interestingly, not everyone wore the same uniform. In another odd twist, the students were often better dressed than the teachers—including me— who mostly wore T-shirts and jeans.

When classes began, I was surprised how easy it was. There were only nine students and everyone had a workbook and textbook. My teacher's edition laid out lesson plans that were easy to follow. We listened to songs and the children glowed when they learned the words enough to sing along. When I read cartoon strips aloud they all laughed. When I finished one little girl would always raise her hand.

"Yes?"

"Teacher. Again please!"

The rest of the class would nod in agreement.

I asked them questions and even when they spoke with each other they mixed their limited vocabulary with hand gestures and body movement.

I asked one boy what his favorite sport was. He stood up, crumbled a piece of paper and put it on the ground in front of him.

"I like . . ." He kicked the paper between two chairs. "Gooaaaallllll!" he yelled.

"You like soccer," I said.

"Yes. You like soccer."

I shook my head and pointed to my chest. "I." I pointed again. "I like soccer." Then I pointed to his chest and said "You like soccer."

He smiled. "Teacher. I like soccer."

I smiled too. I had never thought about teaching before; for me it had been just a job in a faraway place whose only requirement was that I spoke English. In fact, it was just about the only job I was qualified for in Ecuador with my limited language skills and professional experience. It was oddly satisfying though to watch these children learn and grow and know that I played a small part.

*

At the end of my first week of classes I noticed a few people standing in front of the *Universidad de Cuenca*. They had bandanas covering their face and had dragged a pile of tree branches into the road. The next day there were a few more people and two tires were lit on fire in front of the blockade.

Some other expat teachers told me that people were angry with the president. "Something or other about firing the courts or changing his politics."

On the third day of the blockades I sat down on the curb after class to observe. Burning tires had replaced the branches and there were about a hundred people. The police had set up their own blockade down the road. University students in bandanas were pounding the asphalt with large rocks, breaking it into pieces.

I was expecting them to launch the broken asphalt toward the police—and they did. But then, to my surprise, the police started picking up the stones and chunks of road and throwing them back at the protesters. Around the edges, other university students on break from class, their backpacks bulging with textbooks, watched the action unfold. The city oozed with the smell of burning rubber.

Every day the blockade grew a little bigger.

We kept the windows open during class to catch a breeze, and every day we would hear the burst of shotguns firing tear gas canisters into the air. It was like our warning bell and quickly became part of the rhythm of the lesson. By the time the police attacked the blockade, class was almost over. I forced myself to act casually whenever noises from the street invaded our classroom. I just smiled and read the next English cartoon strip as the kids followed along. *Holy shit that sounds like a lot of tear gas. I wonder what's happening out there*, I would think to myself. But my students didn't seem to notice it at all. They were all in elementary school, so either they were too young to understand or had already become accustomed to the noise of a nation in protest.

When I walked home, before I saw or heard anything, I felt the burn in my eyes from the lingering gas in the air. Each day the blockades grew a little larger and lasted a little longer.

*

My school had helped me find a room to rent in the city center. It was small and only had space for a twin-size bed, chair and small desk. The kitchen and bathrooms were all shared. Everyone there was a foreigner. Four of them worked at my school and the other five either worked at other schools or for NGOs. Everyone spoke English.

Two blocks from my front door was *Parque Calderón*, and I spent a lot of my free time there with a book, or a pen and paper. While the park served as the city's main square and was forever bustling with people, I found the space oddly peaceful. Tall evergreens blocked out the worst of the sun and a series of small speakers played soft classical music in the background. The park was sandwiched between an immaculate federal building with crisp flags hanging off its balcony and the *Catedral de la Inmaculada Concepción*. The massive cathedral dominated the cityscape and was the site of a 1985 mass by Pope John Paul II that drew tens of thousands of worshipers from all over the country and was still being talked about when I arrived—which also explained why almost every Ecuadorian male I met in his early twenties was named Juan Pablo.

About two weeks after I arrived in Cuenca I was sitting on a bench in the park when the more moderate counterparts to the student radicals began showing up in large numbers. Lucy, a teenage girl with pigtails sitting next to me, was clearly excited, and she spoke enough English to carry on a conversation.

"What's going on?" I asked. "I mean, I've seen the protests at the university, but I'm in the park every day and I've never seen anything here."

She took her eyes off the growing crowd long enough to smile at me playfully and ask, "You didn't hear?"

She went on without pausing for my response, turning her attention to the crowd again.

"The mayor was on the radio this afternoon and he came out against the president. He told everyone in the city to come to the park to protest."

I kept my eyes on my new friend, who had spent a year in the U.S. as an exchange student. She paused and grinned at me again. She could see how fascinated I was with all of this, how I hung on her every word. She tried to act nonchalant but seemed almost giddy at the chance to explain things to me.

"The government's going to fall," she said.

The crowd chanted, "*¡Fuera Lucio!*—Lucio out!" calling the president by his first name as they marched around the park. More people continued to show up, filling the empty roads that outlined the square, and a crowd massed in front of the federal building. Police in blue-gray camouflage uniforms and military-style hats stood shoulder to shoulder between the building's massive pillars, staring out onto the crowd with emotionless faces.

"Lucio was supposed to be for the people," Lucy told me. "He was supposed to be different, but he just wants money and power. Before he was president he led a revolt of the people. He said the North Americans would have too much influence here. And now look at him!" Her voice rose. "He is trying to sell my country to the Yankees." She seemed very calm, almost distant most of the time, but for short bursts it was clear that she was as angry as everyone else.

In 2000, Ecuador's currency, the sucre, was experiencing rapid inflation. President Jamil Mahuad announced he would abandon the sucre in favor of the U.S. dollar, which upset a lot of people. Besides being seen as a loss of sovereignty, the change would mean that people's savings, the thousands of sucres accumulated over a lifetime, would now only be worth a few dollars. Large street protests erupted across the nation. The Confederation of Indigenous Nationalities of Ecuador (CONAIE) led a march on Congress on January 21st. Then a Lieutenant Colonial in the Ecuadorian army, Lucio Gutiérrez, disobeyed his orders and his unit stood aside and allowed protesters to take over the national parliament. Guiterez joined the protesters' occupation and formed a three-man junta alongside CONAIE president Antonio Vargas and retired

Supreme Court Justice Carlos Solórzano. The three-man junta declared Mahaud's presidency invalid and ruled the nation for three hours. After successfully stripping the president of his power and forcing him to flee the country they peacefully handed power back to Vice President Gustavo Noboa for an interim government. The success was temporary however; a few months later the government went forward with the 'dollarization.' The armed forces also jailed Gutiérrez for his role in the coup, before granting him amnesty after serving four months. With nationwide recognition and the support of a leftist coalition that included the powerful indigenous movement, Gutiérrez was elected president in 2002.

Remembering small pieces of conversations with other teachers and clips from newspaper articles, I asked Lucy a question. "He fired the Supreme Court too, right?"

"Yeah, that was the worst part. He only won the election because all the left parties supported him, but then he abandoned them for the PSC [a conservative political party] and started stealing funds from them to grow his own party. The courts were going to impeach him, so he fired them. He's not even allowed to do that. He's just as corrupt as all the other presidents we have thrown out."

Lucy was still explaining everything to me when a caravan of men in suits arrived.

The mayor and other local politicians walked toward the protesters, waving, expecting to be greeted as heroes. But the chant abruptly changed to "*¡Que se vayan todos!*—They all must go!"

The crowd flowed toward the new arrivals, blocking their path. The politicians immediately turned around and hurried away in their black Mercedes Benzes. As they disappeared behind tinted windows, the crowd roared.

I stayed in the park after Lucy left and continued to observe, fixated by what was happening in front of me. Above the noise, I heard three people loudly chanting something new as they snaked through the street. More people joined them, their voices becoming louder as the moving mass grew more distinct. Dozens strong now, they made their way out of the thick crowd in front of the government building, around the square and back again. By the time they made a full circle around the park the chant had reached a fever pitch and the crowd yelled out in unison, *"¡Todos los dias hasta que Lucio se vaya!*—Every day until Lucio leaves!"

As I was leaving the park I bumped into Peter, a foreign journalist from Ireland covering the protest. His collared shirt was untucked and his red hair was knotted and falling onto his forehead. He stopped to ask me my take on the situation.

"I've only been here a couple of weeks, but I've never felt this energy before," I said.

He had a notepad and pen out but didn't write anything down. "Yeah. I've been to a dozen countries covering civil unrest and protests, but you're right, there's something different going on here—something bigger."

Staring back into the crowd, he invited me for a drink.

"Sure." I said.

He led me to a restaurant a few blocks away. "I had breakfast here this morning. Good food," he said. The menus were in English and other foreigners were scattered around.

"So why Ecuador?" Peter asked after we ordered a couple of *Cuba Libres*.

"It was fairly random actually. I just wanted to live in a place completely different from everywhere else I have known."

"But that's the end of the story. Where does it start? No one picks up and moves across the world without a good reason."

"Ah, well, I suppose the start of the story would be September 11th."

Peter nodded. This was what he wanted to hear. "Were you in New York when it happened?"

"No, I was at school, about two hours away."

"So you saw it on the news?"

"Well my girlfriend called me," I told him. "She didn't even say hello. She just asked which building my dad worked in."

"Even in Ireland it was all anyone was watching," Peter said. He explained how his mom was living in Michigan and he tried calling her but the line was down.

"Same for me. I couldn't call any of my family in New York because the circuits were overloaded."

"Yeah, I remember that. I thought it was part of the attack at first."

I nodded. "Me too. And when I turned on the TV the news was still reporting that other planes were in the air. And in the background people were jumping out of buildings. It didn't feel real."

"Yeah, that day was fucked." Peter tilted back his drink and waved at the waitress for another. "Was your family alright?"

"Yeah. My dad saw the second plane hit and got stranded in Manhattan after the trains shut down. My uncle, who's a cop, was actually at Ground Zero helping people evacuate before the towers collapsed, but he ran fast enough to make it out alright."

"Shit, he was lucky."

"Yeah."

We were moving off track and Peter, ever the journalist, brought us back. "But, how did all that land you here in the middle of these protests?"

"Well, September 11th made me into an activist," I explained. "I wanted to help make a world where that could never happen again."

Peter nodded. "And then the Iraq War and George Bush and all that."

"Yeah. People wanted war. They actually wanted it. September 11th changed a lot of people, and I didn't like those changes." I told Peter how my uncle, the one who escaped the falling towers, spent weeks searching for body parts flung from the planes onto Manhattan rooftops and went to tons of funerals for all the cops who died. "He had it rough, but all he wanted afterward was revenge."

Peter frowned and shook his head as I sipped my beer.

"Everyone was flying American flags," I continued, "but it wasn't patriotism—it was nationalism."

"What do you mean?" Peter asked.

Patriotism is pride in one's nation, I told Peter, but nationalism is the belief that your nation is better than the others and can play by different rules. Nationalism means that you value life in your country above others and that you believe your culture is superior and should replace others, by violence if necessary. It makes us seek vengeance over one death of ours but feel indifference when another nation suffers hundreds of deaths. It makes us think we are always just and innocent and leads to cultural imperialism and war.

Peter nodded. "That's some heavy stuff. In Ireland, we use the word nationalism with a different meaning, but yours makes sense too."

I nodded. "I hated it. I packed my bags as soon as Bush was re-elected."

*

A week after I witnessed the protest in the park with Lucy, I heard about the General Strike. The school I worked at was foreign-owned—Canadian—and only hired foreign, native English speakers to teach. Outside the teachers' lounge was a corkboard that was always filled with photocopied pages from the Lonely Planet or printed out news articles from U.S. newspapers. But that was all taken down. Tacked to the center of the board was a single sheet of paper from the U.S. embassy. It read that the opposition was planning an indefinite general strike for the cities of Quito and Cuenca and that U.S. citizens and businesses may become targets. It warned all Americans to keep a low profile.

A chill of excitement passed through me.

The school didn't wait for the official start of the strike on April 12th; next to the notice from the embassy was another one from the school: all classes were canceled indefinitely.

That afternoon I went with some of the teachers for drinks in place of class. About 3,500 foreigners were living in Cuenca at the time, mostly from North America and Europe, and expat pubs were scattered all over downtown.

We passed a group of men pasting red posters to store windows. The only words I recognized were "STRIKE" and "REVOLUTION" next to the following day's date. There was a pickup truck parked down the road with stacks of thousands of these flyers and people were grabbing piles of them and setting off down different streets.

We ducked into Inca Bar, a popular expat pub downtown and set up at one of the long wooden tables stained with English graffiti.

"We'd better stock up on liquor before tomorrow," joked David, a balding North American in his early thirties. Everyone forced a laugh but the mood was subdued; none of the teachers had ever witnessed a general strike before and the embassy notice had put them on edge.

"If anyone wants to stay with me, there are some extra couches and plenty of room at my place. It's mostly Americans and Germans anyway, so everyone speaks English," said Marisa, a pale skinny woman from Indiana just out of college. "We should stick together."

"It's bad enough we have to walk the long way to class to avoid the university. I hope the country can get its act together soon or I'm leaving," said a second woman I didn't recognize.

I didn't say anything but I was already plotting a long day outside. *I'll go to the park first—and I bet there will be a lot of action near the university.* My beer was more celebration than distraction.

The next morning I walked to the park—it was only five short blocks from my home. Riot police stood in neat lines in front of the government buildings and two tanks were parked on opposite corners with more riot police clustered around them. But that was it. There was not a single protester. In fact there wasn't a single person; just me, some riot police and tanks.

I walked around downtown and it was similarly deserted. I passed a few people on the sidewalk and saw a handful of cars drive by but none of them looked like protesters. Scraps of red paper hung from lines of tape on closed store windows. Someone had ripped down most of the posters.

This is a general strike? Well that was a bit anti-climactic, I thought. I went home for lunch.

In the evening the buses began to run again. It started to look like defeat. I walked down to the university, and there was the usual blockade set-up. There may have been a few extra people than usual but still only a few hundred in total. There was something different though. Normally the students kept the fire fairly small, just big enough to keep the flames going and throw off some smoke. This night, the flames reached over my head. The protesters were burning their reserves. I sat down on the curb behind the main group and took out my notebook.

Despite the fire and slightly larger crowd the space was quieter. It felt like the end of a long party when your own bed starts to seem more attractive than another drink.

A small group broke off from the crowd and walked to a main street nearby where buses had begun to run again. They stopped a bus, made everyone get off and drove it to the barricade where they parked it in front of the line of flames. When people realized what was happening they began to cheer. The masked students walked off the bus and threw the keys into the river. "*¡Viva el paro!*—Long live the strike!" They shouted.

The crowd erupted. Pockets of students broke off and ran to other roads. They hijacked more buses, parked them in intersections and walked away. The mood shifted dramatically. It was the most excited I had ever seen the crowd. People were yelling and dancing in the street.

This would never happen in the U.S., I wrote in my notebook. *People are hijacking buses! And it's not only accepted by everyone here as legitimate but inspires more action and has reenergized the crowd. In the U.S. a person would earn a few years in jail for hijacking a bus, and I'm sure many protesters themselves would condemn the act. Shit, if people had started hijacking buses in Hartford or New York, I might have even told them to stop, and I was way more radical than the average protester there. I might be changing my mind though—I've been too caught up trying to follow the rules and be a 'good' dissident. Real change won't come from within, it didn't back home and it won't here. But now is probably a smart time for me to leave; I'm excited to see what tomorrow brings.*

The next morning there were small crowds in the street and the mood was optimistic. I went to the blockade that was set up in front of the university to try and talk with some of the students. It was the biggest I had ever seen it. I was struggling to speak to a few of them with my mostly non-existent Spanish when a bilingual student came over and began to translate for me. Luis had long black hair and wore a red bandana over his face. He had family in New York and had been visiting them and speaking English from a young age.

"Lucio is a traitor, but they are all traitors," Luis translated his friend for me. "After we throw him out we need a leader who comes from the social movements, someone who isn't part of one of the political parties."

I nodded my head, but before I could reply the first burst of tear gas shot toward us. Police wearing masks had snuck up along the side streets and also charged from the front—a few of them were shooting tear gas pellets from rifles.

I ran with my eyes closed and my lungs burning through clouds of gas and into the university. In Ecuador, police are banned from entering university grounds, which made it a safe zone and the most logical place to put a blockade in front of. I found the group I had been conversing with when the gas chased us apart; I was happy to see some familiar faces in this place where mine didn't fit in. They were standing at the edge of a large concrete sidewalk that extended from one of the university entrances. I nodded my head toward Luis and the others and collapsed onto the grass next to them. A boy of no more than thirteen lit a cigarette, walked around the circle and blew smoke into everyone's eyes.

"It helps take away the gas," Luis told me. The boy bent down, cupped his hands around his mouth and gently exhaled the cigarette smoke onto my eyes. Luis said something I didn't understand to another student in the circle who rummaged through his bag and took out a green bandana. Luis handed it to me, "Put this on and cover your mouth and nose. It helps."

As a water bottle was passed around to wash out our eyes and mouths Luis sat down on the grass and explained to me what was happening. A couple of his friends sat down with us, half paying attention while they rested.

"The blockades start every day around lunch time. They start small and grow through the day; always the same," Luis explained. But that day, he told me, when a few people went out early and started dragging some branches into the road, a car pulled up. When the students approached the car to tell them to go around, several plainclothes police jumped out and started beating the students. They ran into the university for protection but the police followed. Luis added, with more anger, "The police are not allowed here!"

"So what happened?"

Luis pointed a few feet away, past his cousin examining the welt on his stomach where one of the tear gas bullets struck, to the concrete sidewalk. There were fresh blood stains.

"There. That's where the cops caught up to them; that's the student's blood," he said. "Word spread fast after that. Someone came into my class and gave us the news. The class just stopped and a bunch of us ran over here but the injured students were already being helped, so we went out into the street and built the blockade."

The gas lifted while we spoke. The police had taken back the parked buses and retreated. Luis tied a white shirt over his face and we walked back into the street. Other students had already split off to get more buses. Luis picked up two fist-sized rocks as we joined the students who were already blocking the street with their bodies where the bus had stood. With the road cleared a tank began moving toward us. I could feel a slight rumble in the pavement as the tank approached. The engine and gears screeched as they bounced over debris in the road before the sound was drowned out by the clank of rocks smashing against its metal. Luis's eyes stared at me through the hole in his mask. He put one of the rocks in my hand and said, "Fight with us," as his eyes shifted back to the quickly approaching tank.

I had translated an English phrase that I liked before I went to the protest, and even though our conversations had been in English, I read out of my notebook in his language: "*Mis palabras son mi arma*— My words are my weapon." I handed the rock back to Luis.

He nodded his head. I had told him earlier that I wanted to write an article about all this for a U.S. audience. In the next moment he wound up and threw one of the rocks full force. The stone smashed into the metal grating in front of the windshield and bounced off. A dozen more clanks of stone against metal followed as more students let go with their projectiles.

*

A few days later I was in the park chatting with Sonia, another teacher from my school, when families began to arrive for their daily dissent.

Sonia was from Scotland and had frizzy blond hair, a curving body, charming accent and a sense of adventure. She was the only other foreigner I knew who was excited rather than scared by the protests. "This is the kind of thing you read about in other places, so if it happens here I wanna see it," she told me the first time we stopped at the blockade together. We were walking home from school and she was carrying Scrabble with her—a prop from class earlier that day— when we sat down on the curb for a few minutes to watch. "Let's set this up and start playing. Come on now, it'll be fun," she told me. The police tank started barreling our way and we had to hastily throw the board and stray letters into her bag before we could start, but I loved her spirit. She made me feel sane.

Mothers and fathers holding their young children's hands paraded around the park, calling for the resignation of the president. Then, suddenly, hundreds of students from the blockades appeared in commandeered buses; it was the first time these two groups had come together. Before all the students could exit the buses, the police started throwing tear gas grenades into the park. Everyone scattered. Within seconds the entire square was filled with a suffocating cloud and I lost sight of Sonia while trying to escape. I heard her scream before she disappeared into the poisonous fog. Armed with gas masks and long, wooden sticks, the police chased the scurrying groups away from the park and then through the streets. I closed my eyes and ran.

Those first few minutes were extremely chaotic. Tear gas was being fired without pause, police were swinging their three-foot-long batons wildly and beating anyone they could catch. Young children who had come to the park with their families were crying. Some had become separated from their parents and were hysterical.

The type of tear gas the police were using had been developed as a military weapon and was banned in my home country—this felt nothing like getting gassed in Washington D.C. or Boston. Once the gas hit, it felt as if a sharp knife was being scraped against my eyeballs and I reflexively crunched my eyelids closed. After a few seconds my body started to violently dry-heave, as if my lungs were trying to jump out of my chest.

Every few seconds I blinked my eyelids open to orientate myself and each time the scene was worse. The police had stopped tossing the bulky tear gas canisters and started using shotguns that fired large oval bullets of concentrated gas. The bullets didn't travel far, but at close range they were powerful enough to break your ribs. Once fired, the gas shot out into the air through small holes in the bullets. The pressure pushing the gas out was so great that the friction heated up the bullets to the point that they often burst into flames. Most of them bounced off the trees or skipped to a stop on the ground but some of them struck the parents, children and students trying to flee. With my eyes still closed I heard screams behind me, and bullets whizzing past my head.

It was the first time I was scared.

As the police chased us through the streets, the different groups began to find themselves. The initial panic was being replaced with adrenaline. Within an hour the police had retreated and protesters had set up barricades at all the major intersections downtown.

I recognized a student from the university blockade and was able to borrow his phone to try to get in touch with Sonia. She was safe at another seized intersection at the other side of downtown.

At my little occupied intersection, the dissidents made large fires in the streets and danced around the flames. I stayed on the edge, scribbling into my notebook.

Someone had brought a radio out just in time to hear reports that sections of Quito had been overrun by protesters; cases of beer had already been bought at the corner bodega and people sprayed their beer in the air. I stayed on the outside of the action and observed with joyful fascination and a bit of envy, wishing that social movements were as strong and brave in my country. Thirty minutes later the radio reported that the police ring around Congress had been broken and the building occupied by protesters. As the night wore on and fear was fully replaced with excitement, entire families flowed out from their apartments and joined the street parties all over Cuenca. The government would never regain control of the city.

El Universo, the nation's largest newspaper, carried these headlines the next day: *Tres Muertos y 307 Heridos Dejaron las Manifestaciones* (Three Dead and 307 Injured in the Protests); *Estudiantes se Tomaron el Congreso Nacional* (Students Take Congress); *Fotógrafo Chileno Murió Asfixiado* (Chilean Photojournalist Dies of Asphyxiation).

In the morning the national police chief resigned in protest over the heavy-handed tactics of the government. Many local police and military officers walked off the job, and the ones who remained did nothing to stop the protesters from occupying government buildings throughout Cuenca.

That afternoon the president fled the country and his government collapsed.

In the Shadow of a Volcano

The vice president took over, the free trade deal was postponed, the blockades were lifted, and life began to seem more normal. All the notices and newspaper articles that had been tacked to the cork board in the teacher's lounge had been taken down. In their place was a sign-up sheet to help a U.S. government-sponsored development program in a nearby mountain village. Spots were filling up fast but there wasn't a lot of information about what was happening. I asked Steve, the first teacher who had gone, what it was like.

Steve told me he taught a few English classes and the villagers were also learning how to make pizza and hamburgers.

I learned more about the project from others. The small agricultural village was at the end of a road and didn't have a strong connection with Cuenca nor any tourism. The project was designed to make the village more attractive to tourists to generate more income.

It wasn't for me. I had no intention of trying to shape Ecuador into something more familiar. It also seemed a form of cultural imperialism, though I was the only one I knew of at the school who thought that.

Despite having such different reactions to the protests and foreign influence, I fell into a routine of socializing with other teachers and expats. We may have had different opinions on revolution and development, but we still had a lot in common. We were all still 'other' in a foreign land. People treated us differently.

It's easy to notice when you are treated worse than others, but it can be difficult to recognize when people treat you better. It can be even harder to admit it—that your good fortune is not only due to hard work but also a privilege you did nothing to earn. In Cuenca, most foreigners were treated better than locals, myself included. Not everyone treated us better, but many did, whether it was a woman who caught your eye in a bar, or a shop owner who assumed that your underpayment was a mistake, or an employer who hired you based on how you looked. I never thought about it then. It was only much later, when nationalism washed over Ecuador and people started to treat me less favorably that I noticed. Still, even if it was to our collective advantage, being treated differently helped push all of us together. It made us all relate to each other.

As my first ninety days in Ecuador approached I had to plan a trip across the border to renew my visa. I asked around and it seemed most of the other foreigners circumventing official visa policy went to Máncora, a Peruvian beach and popular tourist destination. I went to Tumbes instead. The two cities were in the same corner of northern Peru but I thought it'd be nice to get out of the expat bubble, if only temporarily.

Crossing back over was easy. I handed over my passport and got a stamp with another ninety days. In a way, I was still conforming to the regime of borders. Real defiance would have been throwing away my passport, but that seemed like it would cause much more trouble than it was worth. I actually didn't think about borders much at all. I wanted my first decision in a new chapter of my life to be symbolic of my hypothetical ideal, but the theory of borders faded to the background after that.

Once I returned there wasn't much time left. I had only committed to the school in Cuenca for a ten-week semester and once that ended I decided to do some traveling.

*

Latacunga was a small mountain city of 51,000 people seven hours north of Cuenca. It was just a dot on my map on the way to Quito and when I asked others about it most people gave me a version of the answer, "No one goes there to visit. It's just a town, not a place for tourism." And that sold me on seeing it for myself.

I arrived late at night and went straight to sleep in the first hostel I saw. In the morning I walked to the roof to try to get a view of the place. As soon as I stepped out I saw it: Cotopaxi, the world's tallest active volcano, was just a few miles northeast of the city. Later I would learn that the summit was almost always covered in clouds, but that morning the snow-capped peak stood in sharp contrast against the blue sky.

Cotopaxi is thrice the height of the mile-high city of Denver at 19,347 feet (5,897 meters) but it wasn't just tall; it was massive. The summit was covered with over one thousand feet of glacial ice that had built up since the last major eruption in 1877.

The city lived and died with the volcano. Glacial ice melt poured down the mountain and formed *Río Cutuchi*, which split Latacunga in half and provided a constant supply of fresh water. Past eruptions also filled the area's soil with nutrients and the volcano itself trapped clouds in its orbit creating a micro-climate with plenty of moisture. Cotopaxi helped make the region ideal for different types of agriculture, from roses to potatoes to a special kind of tomato that grew on a tree. Latacunga was in the center of it all and acted as a commercial trading hub.

But Cotopaxi also destroyed the city. There might be a break of a hundred years or more between eruptions, but when Cotopaxi did erupt it was devastating. Thrice in recorded history—in 1744, 1768 and 1877— major lava eruptions melted the volcano's glacial ice cap. The flash flood mixed with volcanic ash and gravel to form a sort of tidal wave of wet cement that followed the small valley carved by *Río Cutuchi* and leveled everything in its path, including most of Latacunga, just 15 miles away. Each time, the city was rebuilt.

We were a short drive away from the center of the earth—the equator—but the air was brisk on the rooftop that morning. The tropical latitude was nearly canceled out by the high elevation and gave the place a sense of permanent spring. Spring has always been my favorite season.

I walked outside the hotel and into a bustling market. Broccoli and carrots were spread across rows of tables, buckets were filled with garlic and potatoes, and bananas and mangos were piled in giant pyramids of tropical fruit trucked in from the coast. Behind each pile of produce was a woman with calloused hands, long black hair, and rosy cheeks. Other women meandered through the crowd, calling out whatever they had: *"¡Diez aguacates, un dólar! ¡Diez aguacates, un dólar!"* All of it smelled like my parents' vegetable garden after a late summer rain.

When I bought my plane ticket to Ecuador I didn't think much about the indigenous culture. It wasn't something that ever came up. There was barely a mention of South America in all my cumulative years of history class and I had no idea how vibrant indigenous culture was in the Andes. They had largely held onto a culture and language that existed before the Europeans came, back to when they were part of the Incan empire. While nearly everyone had converted to Catholicism it was a different breed from what I was used to, mixed with their previous belief system that had worshiped nature. Quechua, the Andean indigenous language, was widely spoken in Latacunga and many of its words were mixed into the local Spanish dialect as well. In fact, the city's name was a fusion of Quechua and Spanish. The indigenous called the original settlement 'tacunga' and the Spanish added the article 'la' when they arrived, and they eventually merged into one word. 'Cotopaxi' is a Quechua word which means 'throat of fire.' The name 'Andes' came from the Quecha word *anti*, which means 'where the sun rises.'

In Cuenca I had learned that the countryside was majority indigenous, but Latacunga was the first city I saw with such a strong indigenous presence. Perhaps that was it though; Latacunga didn't feel like a city, it felt like a village. It felt like a clean break from the life I left behind in New York.

I wandered farther from the market through the narrow cobblestone streets. Storefronts were not always in a uniform line and occasionally they cut into the sidewalk, making the pedestrian path so thin that you had to step into the street when someone came from the other direction. It was clearly a town built before cars. After a few minutes, I stumbled upon *Parque Vicente León* and sat down. Like the central park in Cuenca, this one was sandwiched between government buildings and a church but the buildings were far less impressive here. "¡*Fuera Oxy! Fuera TLC!*—No Oxy [A U.S. oil company]! No Free Trade Agreement!" was spray-painted on the Federal building's façade. Both buildings had patches of new paint that didn't quite match the base color—half-hearted attempts of erasing past graffiti. *Vicente León* was also much more open than its Cuenca counterpart. There were a few small trees but most of the park was covered in sun rather than shade. The buildings blocked many of the surrounding mountains, but a few of the taller peaks could be seen reaching above the rooftops.

I already liked Latacunga, so when I sat down in *Vicente León*, I was probably just looking for an excuse to stay longer. That's when I made my first friend. Veronica had long brown hair, and while her lips shined with gloss and her eyes hid behind too much blue powder, she wore a plain green shirt and her backpack looked worn. Two years later our friendship would come to an abrupt and bitter end, but regardless, she played an oversized role in my life in Latacunga by making small introductions that would have large consequences. I was writing in my notebook when she sat down. She looked forward and kept silent, but a minute later when I paused my writing and looked up, she spoke.

"*Hola.*"

She smiled at me. She knew a few words of English and we struggled patiently to converse in a mix of our languages.

"What do you do?" she asked.

Two young boys, each carrying a small wooden box and a hard-bristled brush, stopped a few feet in front of us and stared.

"I'm an English teacher," I said.

The two boys walked away, following a businessman as he walked by and asking if he wanted his shoes shined.

"Oh, really? Why don't you come work at my university? It's one of the best in the country," Veronica said.

"I don't think I'm qualified for that."

She looked confused, and I wondered if she just didn't understand my English. "You can work there. It's close, I can take you there now. Why not?"

I smiled at Veronica's question. Ecuador had infused me with the sense that anything was possible. I repeated her last words, though not loud enough for Veronica to hear. "Why not?"

The university was on a busy street and only a few blocks south of the park. The building itself had a fresh coat of white paint. Stone steps lead to massive mahogany doors that served as the main entrance. On either side were stained glass windows.

Directly above the doors the two-story building rose steeply upward toward a point. The tower was much higher than the rest of the building, or any building in the neighborhood in fact. It reminded me of a cathedral. Veronica knew her way and led me down the long, stone-tiled hallway, to a row of offices.

"We are here," she said and walked inside one of the offices.

I followed her in.

"*Perdón, tengo un amigo estadounidense aquí. Él es profesor de inglés y está interesado en trabajar aquí. ¿Puede hablar con la directora?*" Veronica's words came out too fast for me to catch them all but the three or four people working in the office all looked up, then looked at me. One man smiled and stood up.

"Hello! Very nice to meet you." He came over and shook my hand while speaking near-perfect English. "I'll be right back with the Director. Please take a seat."

Veronica smiled and grabbed my notebook from my hand. She wrote down her phone number on the first page. "We meet soon," she said before kissing me on the cheek and walking away.

I barely had time to sit down before the Director came in. She was tall and was wearing a navy-blue pant suit. "You are interested in working here? Come, follow me."

I stood up and followed her to a desk and two chairs in the far corner of the room.

The interview was short. Within an hour of meeting Veronica in the park I was offered a job. Ecuador was a whirlwind of adventure. I felt like a twig that had fallen into a surging river. The current twisted and turned and I let it carry me onward, enjoying all the views along the way.

"We'll take care of everything for you here. Just come on the first day of the semester and we'll give you housing and you'll be able to eat in the cafeteria as well—all paid for."

And like that, half a year after I finished an undergraduate degree in media studies and sociology I had become a college professor at one of the nation's most prestigious universities—in a field in which I barely had any experience in and in a nation whose language I still couldn't speak.

I had a few days before classes started so I continued my trip and revisited Quito before returning to Latacunga for the start of the new semester. When I arrived for my first day of work, two men in army fatigues took my duffel bag out of my hand.

I must have looked confused.

Another English teacher whom I had seen during my interview but to whom I had not been formally introduced smiled at me. "Don't worry; just go with them for now."

The military men walked off with my bag.

"But … What? What are they doing?"

"Go! Go! They'll bring you back here in a minute. Don't worry."

Still confused, I followed my duffel bag out of the university through a back entrance and crossed the street into a military barracks. A soldier holding a machine gun saluted us and opened a razor wire gate. One of my escorts opened an apartment and set my bag down on the bed in the far room. I picked it back up.

"What are you doing?"

"*Este es su departamento.*"

"Huh?"

He pointed at me then pointed at the bed and spoke slowly. "*Su casa.*" I knew enough Spanish to realize he was trying to telling me this was my house.

"What? No. I don't live here. I don't want to live here. I'll find my own place."

The second man shook his head and motioned for me to put the bag back down on the bed. *"Deje su maleta aquí por favor y regresaremos a la directora ahora. Ella puede contestar cualquier pregunta que tenga."*

"What? I just . . . I'm just a teacher. Why am I here? Do you speak English?"

He motioned for me to follow him and said, *"Aquí es su habitación y màs tarde le mostraré la cantina donde nosotros comemos."*

I stood in the room for a few extra seconds. There were no windows, the walls were painted a dull orange, and the only furnishing besides the bed was a dirty carpet that matched the walls and stunk like a wet dog in need of a bath.

When I got back to the university, my new boss explained that while my students would be civilian, the university was run by the military. The university, called ESPE, was short for *Escuela Politécnica del Ejército*. As it turns out, *ejército* means army.

ESPE was founded in 1922 as a military school that specialized in engineering. In 1972 it began admitting civilians and transitioning into a private university. By the time I arrived almost all the students and faculty were civilian except for a small group of segregated classes of military engineering students and the top administration officials.

"Why didn't you tell me this before?" I asked.

"The Dean is a military officer but that's not important, it's a normal university. I didn't think it would matter to you."

I was fleeing a life in New York in large part because I hated what I perceived as the militarization of everyday life and the acceptance of perpetual war. How could I politely articulate that the idea of living in a military barracks was repulsive?

"I'm going to find a different place to live." I told her.

*

My experiences in Cuenca had been fairly sheltered because of the job I held and the company I kept. When I went out, it was usually with my housemates or coworkers to drink beer, speak English, and marvel at our own greatness for being able to live in such a different place all on our own.

I cannot think of a smoother transition to life in Ecuador than the one I had in Cuenca, revolution and all. Almost everyone finds comfort in community and Cuenca was great for that. There was always someone who had a similar experience, someone to lend advice, someone who understood. Part of the draw of Latacunga for me had been the simple fact that no other foreigners lived there and I would be forced out of my comfort zone.

My experiences in Cuenca were filled with hey-isn't-it-weird-that-they-do-that-here bonding, but not so in Latacunga. Shortly after I arrived I learned that since there were no scheduled garbage pick-ups the municipal trucks would play a song to let everyone know they were coming and to ready their garbage. The song was already familiar to me; it was the same one that ice cream trucks played in the U.S. "Isn't that weird?" I would ask after explaining the irony that the song that I identified with dessert meant waste disposal in Latacunga.

No one ever thought it was weird. I stopped asking.

*

I hated walking through the barbed wire gates to come home to the housing the university had provided. I hated seeing the solider standing there with a gun every day. When I opened my apartment, I walked straight to my room and shut myself in. The common bathroom did not have a door and the only time I saw the two soldiers I shared the apartment with was when I was sitting on the toilet or naked in the shower.

A few days after I moved in I became ill from drinking the water and had severe diarrhea. The plumbing system throughout Ecuador used smaller pipes so that flushing toilet paper would clog and cause the soiled water to flow back out. Next to the toilet I piled feces-stained paper into an overflowing bucket. I never spoke with the soldiers, but they slowed their step at the open bathroom door, staring in on the strange new foreigner occupying their toilet.

Attached to the shower head was a plastic casing the size of my fist with wires running out of it. The water was heated with electricity—the same as I had seen in Cuenca. But there was something wrong with my shower in Latacunga. Every few minutes something would catch and a jolt of electricity would pulse through the water and shock me. It was always just a fraction of a second but I never knew when it would happen and my body would tense up as soon as I turned on the water. The two soldiers took their towels and soap next door; but I had no place else to go.

I met Veronica again but had trouble making friends, in large part because of my poor language skills. I spent time walking around the city or sitting in the park reading when I was feeling well, but that wasn't very often. I probably had a calorie-deficiency because I was consuming less meat and much of what I did eat turned to diarrhea as my body adjusted to the water.

There was an issue at the university and my workload was reduced to a single class. I taught 'conversation' and enjoyed moderating and encouraging discussion. It was usually the best part of my day. But after class, for lack of anything better to do or lack of energy, I would walk across the street into the military barracks and struggle to make sense of the Spanish-language newspapers I was trying to learn from.

I considered giving up. I thought about catching a bus to Quito and getting on the next plane to New York. All the things that drove me away from the United States were still there, but just about anything else looked attractive compared to the view from the toilet seat in the military barracks. The thoughts never lasted long, but for fleeting moments the most powerful emotion I felt was solitude and it made me long for the familiar.

*

Three weeks after I began working at the university there was a knock on my bedroom door. It was a man I had met in the park two days previous. His name was Kleaber (pronounced 'clever') and he was wearing jeans and a second-hand suit. A collared shirt was tucked into the jeans, just the same as the first day we met. Though he was only a few years older than me he combed his black hair over his forehead to try and cover a quickly receding hairline.

"Hello John! How are you doing?!" he said with a little too much gusto. Kleaber had taught himself English and spoke it perfectly—even better than many professors at the University level.

"Umm. I'm alright." After a brief pause I continued. "How did you find me?"

"Well you said you worked at ESPE so I went there and asked around for you." He poked his head into the doorway. "May I come in?"

"Oh, okay," I said, still somewhat surprised at my first visitor. "Sure, come in."

"I have a business proposition for you." He sat on the couch in the foyer. It was the first time I ever saw anyone sit there.

"Sure," I said, and sat down in a wooden chair across from him.

Kleaber ran a one-man English school. He organized classes, tutored individuals and would help with homework. He had even dressed in disguise and taken proctored exams at various schools. Anything for the right price.

"I have two students who want to learn from a native speaker. The pay is pretty good—would you be interested?"

I agreed out of boredom as much as anything else but the prospective students never turned up and I never taught them. Still, Latacunga was small enough that I would bump into Kleaber quite often. He would confirm an answer on a difficult homework question or ask me to define a new word he saw on a message board he visited online. I had questions for him too. Which bus to take; how much things cost; and where to find certain markets. Often this would happen while I was sitting in the park, either reading or watching the town walk by. When I ran into him near the main food market one day he invited me to meet his mother and have coffee.

Two blocks north of the market we turned toward the cemetery. On one corner a woman stood behind a yellow tank of gas that connected to a stove-top. She was frying empanadas in a giant wok. Across from her another woman was grilling what looked like sausages. Beyond them, lining the north side of the street, vendors had set up flower displays on homemade wooden tables that sat where cars would have otherwise parked.

After walking a few paces past the women selling food on the corner, Kleaber's mother saw us. She had been sitting on the step that lead into her shop but jumped up and waved her hands excitedly and shouted, "*¡Ven! ¡Ven!*"

Her name was Hilda, but I always knew her as *la Señora*. She invited us in to her crowded shop. "Sit down! Sit down!"

She ran off through what appeared to be a hole in the wall and I heard her turn on the stove. *La Señora* was a country girl and she was as tough as her calloused feet.

"She's had this shop my whole life," Kleaber told me.

Bunches of dried flowers hung on wooden sticks and dangled above. The space was only about ten feet by twenty, but it fit a lot. The cushioned bench Kleaber and I were sitting on served as *la Señora*'s bed. There was a pile of blankets in the corner behind a glass case that held dried floral arrangements. Kleaber was sleeping there temporarily and English workbooks poked out from underneath the blankets.

La Señora came back with coffee and ran off again. When she returned she handed me a plate of eggs fried in too much salt. "*¡Cómetelo!*— Eat it!" she shouted at me and then started laughing. I barely understood anything she said, but her enthusiasm and constant laughter at her own jokes in a non-stop monologue was oddly pleasant.

Kleaber's sister Ana stopped by to say hello. She had dyed red hair and wore black leather boots that nearly reached up to her knees.

"Ana also has a store on this block." Kleaber told me. The five brothers and sisters had grown up helping out in their mother's shop next to the cemetery and three of them now owned their own flower shops on the same street. Kleaber had to meet a prospective student and ran off, leaving me with half a cup of coffee I still had to finish.

"I teach English also and would prefer practice if you like my store," Ana said.

Her English, like most teachers I met in Latacunga, was lacking, but it was still much better than my Spanish.

She gave me a seat in her shop and she sat opposite me on a cross section from a large tree. The stump was about a foot tall and still had bark on the edges.

"What do you opinion George Bush?" she asked me.

I laughed. "George Bush …" I paused as if I was searching for the right word. I already knew her answer to the question and knew what she hoped I would say. It was always one of the first things Ecuadorians asked me and thus far everyone who had queried had shared my strong dislike for the U.S. president, but I let Ana hang for a second. "George Bush is a donkey."

Ana laughed out loud. I had recently learned that calling someone a *burro*, a donkey, was a strong insult. "George Bush is a donkey; the politicians here are *burros* also."

We chatted more and I yawned. The mountain air was thinner than I was used to. I later learned that yawning happens when your body wants more oxygen, which explains why I sometimes found myself yawning randomly when I first moved to Latacunga. Though, at the time I had no idea why.

"Do you have hunger?" Ana asked.

"No, why?"

"Because you yawned. That means you're hungry."

"Really? Doesn't it mean you're tired?"

"Are you tired?"

"No."

"So you're hungry then?"

"I'm neither hungry nor tired. Sometimes I just yawn."

She smiled and gave her head a slight shake as if she knew I was just being polite. "I'll return fast; I think there's rice I heat you for."

"Seriously, I'm not hungry."

But she was already heading down the street to use the kitchen her mother had just made me eggs in.

*

A month after I moved into the military barracks, Kleaber spoke to the university on my behalf and helped me find a room to rent.

The room was simple and I liked that. It had been an unused alcove between two other bedrooms above a street-side restaurant. With my deposit the landlord bought wood and nails and built a wall out of plywood and two by four lumbers to create my room. He showed me what paint he already had and I chose to cover my windowless room in sky blue. An old bed and dresser, collecting dust in the space before the fourth wall was built, stayed and became my own.

There was a community kitchen across from my new room, a communal bathroom down the hall and a concrete basin with running water on the roof for washing clothes. I immediately set about teaching myself how to cook.

In Cuenca, while I was contemplating borders and deciding to begin my new life ignoring their authority, I also started to think about food differently. In the markets, freshly killed chickens hung upside down in clear plastic bags. They were already plucked of their feathers, often by dipping their body in boiling water, sometimes while still alive, but everything else was still intact. Blood drained from their lifeless body through a slit in their neck and pooled in the corner of the bag. In the countryside outside of Cuenca I had my first up close experience with cows and helped a friend yank a baby calf away from its mother—so there would be more milk to sell. The week-old calf desperately struggled to stay close, ignoring the rope tied around its neck that we pulled it away with.

Henry David Thoreau's message from *Civil Disobedience*—that when you oppose an unjust system the true revolutionary act is not to fight against it and lend legitimacy through recognition of its authority, but to completely withdraw from it—guided me not just with borders but with everything I tried to do in my new life. In the U.S. I had been disturbed by the treatment of animals that would eventually end up on our dinner plates. I made sure to avoid veal and always buy cage-free eggs, and hoped that would help bend things in a more humane direction. In Ecuador, I decided to walk away completely. I stopped eating meat.

None of the Ecuadorians I met understood why I chose to remove myself from a system that boiled chickens alive and choked calves trying to stay with their mother, and only the rare vegetarian restaurant would serve a meal I could eat, but I was learning quickly that Ecuador, with its tropical coast, cool mountains and year-round growing season, had excellent food for me, if I only learned to prepare it all myself.

*

Life had never seemed as raw as it did my first few months in Ecuador. Many of the accepted norms that I had grown up with seemed to no longer apply. My paychecks never arrived on time and despite having plans, my new acquaintances would show up late or not at all. The foreign language director would schedule a meeting and arrive an hour late without a word. For months I refused to get a cell phone because I wanted to break from consumerism and have as few possessions as possible, so I relied on meeting people at specific places and times—which was a horrible idea in a land where everyone was always late. Intersections often didn't have stop signs or traffic lights and I didn't know how to cross through the steady traffic. Prices in the market and many stores were unmarked and since I didn't yet know to haggle, I was always overcharged.

I had crossed my first border many months earlier, on an airplane flying into the sprawling capital, but it took moving to Latacunga to feel the new world and really breathe in its nuances. Over the coming years, as I adjusted to a new culture and set of priorities, I began to like these norms more than the ones I had grown up with, but in the beginning, I was, like most cross-border travelers, judging a new place by an old standard. I didn't yet understand that one wasn't better or worse, just different. As time progressed, I would stop to talk with a neighbor I saw on one corner and then a friend's cousin on the next, caring more about the small human joys we shared in casual conversation than the meetings I was already late for, and finally, I began to understand. But my appreciation for community and everyday changes in perception developed slowly. For the most part early on, I was just frustrated. Then I met Lucía.

Mi Amor

In September, when Latacunga was still a strange and foreign place, Veronica told me she had a friend she wanted to set me up with.

"Sure," I said.

Veronica smiled. "*Te va a gustar*—You're going to like her. She used to study industrial psychology with me in Ambato [a city an hour south of Latacunga]." Veronica paused before adding, "She has a child and doesn't go out much, so she needs some fun tonight."

We went to a bar down the street from my house. I was sitting at a table with Veronica and her date, Dan, when Lucía walked in. She had dyed-blond hair and was wearing tight black pants and a pink designer shirt that said 'New York' across the front. She was beautiful, but I immediately knew that she was not for me. She looked shallow and superficial. Before we ordered the second round I had already judged her. She drank too much, wore too much makeup, had too many secrets with Veronica, and I regretted coming out. But, as the night dragged on and the glasses emptied, I began to notice a certain innocence within her.

We ordered a hookah and Lucía inhaled the smoke and choked until she laughed. She had never tried it before. When she did it better the second time, her eyes lit up and she smiled like a child that had just learned a new skill. She was two years older than me at twenty-five but she had the sweet wonder of someone much newer to the world than I, like she had been frozen from reality for years and was just beginning to thaw.

"*¿Quieres probar?*—You want to try?" She asked as she passed me the pipe. Her fingers touched mine.

A pulse of warmth passed through me and we caught each other's eyes. I smiled and let my mouth open partway but no words came out. Lucía touched my hand again, this time on purpose.

"Is it hard for you to live here without speaking Spanish fluently?" She was looking straight into my eyes.

"Sometimes, but sometimes keeping things simple keeps it closer to the truth." I smiled. "What do you like to do?"

"Dance. I love to dance, but I also love my career. I want to figure out what's wrong with people so they can be better." Her body leaned in, just slightly.

When I told her I briefly lived in Cuenca her eyes lit up. She grabbed my idle hand resting on the table, placing her palm over the back and curling her fingers around mine. She gave a quick squeeze. "I was born in Cuenca! Isn't it a wonderful city?"

When the bar closed we all went back to my place to have one last drink in a small common area near my bedroom. I was exhausted and told Veronica, Lucía and Dan that they could stay as late as they wanted but I was going to bed.

A minute later there was a knock on my door. It was Lucía.

"We're leaving now and I wanted to say goodbye," she said. She kissed me, but pulled back suddenly.

"I might not be able to come back to Latacunga for a while, but I'm glad we met tonight." She seemed sad but it was just a flash before her eyes sparkled and she kissed me again, pulling me closer and harder than before.

*

Lucía got my email address from Veronica and sent me a message a few days later.

"I've been thinking of you. I hope I'm on your mind as well. I was wrong, I can come back to Latacunga this week. I want to see you."

On our second date we bought ice cream and walked to a park at the edge of the city. On our way we passed a man lying on the sidewalk, clutching a half empty bottle of *puro*—cane liquor. His jacket and jeans were caked in mud and he had dried blood on his forehead. I walked right past him. Lucía stopped and crouched down next to him.

"*¡Hola!*" Her voice was cheery. She was smiling and gave a small wave. "Hey, how are you doing?"

The man mumbled as he tried to sit up.

Lucía reached out and grabbed his coat by the shoulder and helped him up.

"Arecely," he grunted. "Are you Arecely?" He squinted at Lucía.

"No, my name is Lucía. What's your name?"

"Edwin. My name's Edwin."

"Edwin. It's nice to meet you." Her voice held a constant cheer. Her smile never left.

"I think I fell down."

"Are you hurt?"

Edwin thought for a second, stretched out his legs and looked up at the sky. "No. I think I'm okay." He seemed surprised.

"Well it's sunny out here, you must be thirsty." She took out a fresh water bottle from her bag. "Here, take this."

I had been watching the whole time but didn't say anything. I'm not even sure Edwin knew I was there. When Lucía stood up and we continued walking I asked her. "Why did you stop for that man?"

"Because sometimes life is hard," she said matter-of-factly. "And he looked like he needed someone to be his friend."

We started dating regularly and Lucía would make the trip to Latacunga twice a week.

"I could go to Ambato some days too," I offered.

"No!" She forced a smile. "I like to get away, plus I get to see Veronica here."

"What made you move there anyway?"

Her face dropped and she looked down at her feet. "That's

where *he* is from." Her voice was low. I didn't know how to respond, so I kept quiet. She continued. "I moved there before I had my child and even though my son lives with his father now, I want to be close to him. That's why I'm still there."

"So do you live alone?" I asked.

She looked up at me with large round eyes, and I saw that they were glistening with moisture, ready to spill down her cheeks. "I don't want to talk about it."

I learned not to press for details but sometimes she would casually drop small pieces of her past into conversation and I thought I understood a little more each time. I didn't mind; in fact, I was attracted to it. I wanted to start over too.

*

After a few weeks she began spending the night with me in my sky-blue bedroom. The days when I was sick on the toilet inside a military bunker were long gone. I was happy. Spending so much time with Lucía also helped my Spanish; I was haggling in the markets and having more complex conversations.

Lucía was a magnet for people in need. She had a constant stream of micro-interactions with alcoholic old men or kids working on the street. She would often just smile and wave, but it always seemed to leave people a little happier.

But there was a darker side that began to emerge too. Whenever details of her past were inconsistent, she would tilt her head down and look up at me, showing me the white in her eyes, and drawing me in, silently urging me to help her overcome everything. We both knew there was something deeper lurking, but I was content to wait until she was ready to share everything.

Latacunga was a small enough place that I began to recognize people on the street pretty often when Lucía and I would go for a walk. Lots of my students from the university would stop to chat. About half the time they were female. Often these interactions passed without incident. But not always.

"This is my girlfriend Lucía," I would say. And Lucía would smile and kiss my friend's cheek.

We would all say goodbye and usually that would be it. But sometimes Lucía would wait until we were alone and yell in a quick burst of emotion.

"Everyone always cheats on me and I knew you would too! I saw the way she looked at you!" A minute later she would apologize and forget about the whole thing. This habit surfaced even more strongly when she drank, and occasionally would turn into a small fight. It always left me a little bewildered, how quickly things could turn. But her emotional intensity didn't scare me away, it drew me closer. Her gloom and rage was a quick thunderstorm that inspired more awe than fear and made me appreciate the long periods of sunshine that much more.

For my own part, as much as I liked Ecuador and my new home, I wasn't always happy. In my quest to understand a new place, sometimes I just felt alone. From time to time, a deep solitude gripped me, and threatened to ruin everything else. But once I met *mi amor*, it all went away: she filled all the voids in my life. We knew that we were stronger together than apart. In the frigid face of adversity, we were each other's warmth. We held each other through the parties and the rain. We woke with our naked bodies curled together.

I had dated the same woman for my entire four years at university, but compared to the romance with Lucía, everything before began to seem very casual. She was the first woman I loved. At what was a very intense time in my life, she made everything better. She seemed connected to everything good. Real or imagined, Lucía and the relationship we shared began to represent everything I wanted in life: she was my tomorrow.

*

A few months after Lucía and I started dating we went away together for a long weekend. We traveled on winding roads down the eastern slopes of the Andes. The mountains dropped off rather quickly and yielded to another stunning scene: the Amazon rainforest.

I spent a lot of time riding buses around Ecuador, partly because of how much I enjoyed just looking out the window. Most buses had televisions and at first I was surprised how frequently they showed Jean-Claude Van Damme movies, but I suppose that jump-kicking bad guys doesn't need translation.

The real entertainment for me was to the left and to the right, on the other side of the windows. Unlike in the U.S., the highways were never walled off or hidden. The traffic slowed and the roadside filled with shops and restaurants when it cut through the center of cities and towns. A cluster of vendors waited to board the bus and sell their wares. There were always staples like Coca-Cola, potato chips and even freshly cooked meals of chicken and rice, the heat steaming out of their grey plastic containers. Each place had local specialties as well.

"This is Pelileo," Lucía announced after we passed Ambato and approached the next town.

"What do they have here?" I asked.

"This is where I come to buy jeans. Look." She pointed out the window at a row of shops, all of them selling jeans.

"No, I mean what kind of food. I'm hungry."

She smiled. "Wait, I'll show you."

As the bus slowed I could see half a dozen giant woks lined up. Men and women were rolling dough and putting it into the pan. The odd thing was they weren't using any oil. The first vendor jumped on and Lucía flagged him over.

"Give me one, please."

The man handed over a plastic bag filled with what looked like little pieces of bread. It was difficult to see because the bag was clouded with heat and steam. The bread was fresh.

Lucía tore the bag open and handed one of the pieces to me. I bit in and burned my mouth on a thick brown liquid in the center.

"It's good. What is this?" I asked.

"They cook it with panela inside until it melts." Panela is a raw form of sugar, dark brown and not as sweet. It was sold in solid wheels that weighed a few pounds each in the markets.

We ate the whole bag before they could cool.

Outside Pelileo, we began our descent on winding roads along steep mountains whose peaks were so high they held ice year-round. At the will of the mountainside it was built upon, the road was filled with blind turns and didn't permit any mistakes. Powder blue hearts were painted on the asphalt wherever there'd been a death, and around some curves you would see dozens of them stacked next to each other—a whole bus that had tumbled down the hill.

The area we were driving through was arid and inhospitable to trees. The steep slopes simply appeared yellow from a distance, but up close you could see a thousand clumps of dried grass, holding the dust down and waiting for the next rain. About an hour after turning east and heading down the valley that *Río Pastaza* follows, *Tungurahua*, a highly active volcano, juts into the clouds. Shortly before our trip, the volcano had erupted and the lava flowed over the highway leaving it impassable for several weeks. The road was an important one, and one of the only links between the Andes and Amazon, so the government was quick to send out bulldozers once the lava stopped flowing. The heavy machines scraped off the jagged top layers of igneous rock and flattened the surface enough to make it drivable, leaving the leftover black rock as the biggest and most spectacular speed bump I had ever seen.

Once we returned to the pavement the scenery changed dramatically. We had dropped enough in elevation that, while the slopes were still steep, they were beginning to come alive. There was no firm border between these two very different environments, and they began to blend into each other. As we descended farther it became wetter and hotter. Water dripped down the walls and nourished the small green plants that had replaced the yellowing grasses. Dropping farther, the plants grew larger and thicker, and before long, a dozen different varieties of orchids, each with brilliant colors that filled the spectrum from red to violet, emerged between the bright green leaves. Continuing down, giant leaves of the split-leaf philodendron crowded the ground and turned it a dark green, while red bromeliad flowers poked through. Mokara Orchids dotted the roadside, attracting tiny hummingbirds to the droplets of rainwater around their orange blossoms. Down and down we went until the decline became more gradual, the mountains faded to hills, and the hills became sloping fields. As the earth leveled out, great trees began to push through the green undergrowth and reach into the sky. Finally, we were in the Amazon rainforest.

Lucía had spent much of her youth in a jungle outpost at the edge of the world's largest rainforest, and I had grown up on another continent idealizing the famous river basin, so our first trip together was a natural choice. We arrived at our destination, Tena, with enough time to walk around and eat before going out.

On our first morning we walked across a wooden bridge to an open-air zoo located on an island. The city was divided in two by the massive *Río Tena*, a tributary to the mighty Amazon River, and the island was in the middle of this flowing water. At the end of the bridge sat a middle-aged woman with long messy hair collecting an entrance fee. She tried to charge me extra since I was obviously a foreigner. "But he is my husband. He is Ecuadorian," Lucía protested before I even had a chance to reply. The woman looked at me again, then at Lucía, and we just smiled at each other as she charged us the entrance fee for two nationals.

We held hands and walked onto the island as if on our honeymoon.

We spent the entire day exploring the island. The flora was incredible; everything not only looked other-worldly, but also had a fascinating backstory. All along the trails were the bizarre-looking socratea trees, also known as 'walking palms.' The trees grew three or four feet above the forest floor, held up by a dozen stilt-like roots that formed a triangular dome. This protected the trees from seasonal floods, but even more incredibly, it allowed the trees to travel. The stilts grew quickly and if a large tree had fallen that allowed more sunlight to shine down in one direction all the new stilts would grow toward the light while the stilts on the far side would die off. The tree, albeit slowly, literally walked to better locations throughout its life.

The fauna was also stunning. One of the spider monkeys that roamed free took a liking to us and followed us everywhere we went; swinging through trees, wrapping his calloused tail around my neck, or sitting on my shoulders as he picked bugs and berries from the lowest branches and snacked.

By day we explored everything green, and by night we drank gin and tonics at riverside tiki bars between my dance lessons from Lucía. She loved to dance; she lived for it. I did not, but she was teaching me and with her at my side I was beginning to grow fonder of that ubiquitous part of Latin culture.

After three days we needed to return to the mountains for school and work. On the way to the bus station I saw Lucía yawn.

"*¿Tienes hambre?*—Are you hungry?" I asked.

"Yeah, a little."

We stopped at a small restaurant and I ordered a side of rice and French fries. Being a strict vegetarian severely limited what I could eat outside of my own kitchen. Unless you were in the capital or a tourist hotspot, there were no menus or choices but rather just 'breakfast,' 'lunch' or 'dinner' courses that centered around some kind of meat. Chicken was the most popular, but it wasn't just a drumstick on the side of your plate; every part of the animal was used in each part of the dish. The soup that accompanied every meal was often little more than leftover parts boiled in water: toes, kidneys, bones, and so on. If pork was served, there might be deep fried chips of skin. But if you were really lucky, you got guinea pig, which was considered a delicacy. The animal I once raised as a pet was impaled on a metal rod that tore through its asshole and exited through its mouth, then roasted over a fire.

I had grown accustomed to surviving on side dishes when I ate out. Having little more to eat than rice and potatoes for the weekend did not come as a surprise to me, but Lucía's order did:

rice and potatoes. While we were waiting for the food, she rather matter-of-factly declared: "I won't eat meat anymore. When I'm with you, I will be vegetarian."

We had never spoken about this before. "Really?" I asked.

"Yeah, I didn't realize how hard it was for you before, but now we can do it together." She looked up at me and smiled.

We never spoke of it again, but she kept her word. In my strange new world she was always the woman who was holding my hand—and that meant everything to me.

Where the Sun Rises

Lucía held my heart, but my attachment to my new home was much deeper than just a romance.

My Spanish was improving and I was having real, complex conversations which helped connect me to the place. One of my favorite linguistic idiosyncrasies was rather simple: how people used the word '*vecino*' or 'neighbor.' People called almost everyone *vecino*, whether they lived on the same block or worked in a restaurant across town that they visited once a month. Basically, anyone you recognized became *vecino* or often *veci* for short. People began to greet me on the street by calling out *veci*; and it started to feel as if these people really were my neighbors.

Each night, I returned briefly to English, when I taught a conversation class at the university and began by casually asking my students whatever I wanted to learn about.

"What is happening tomorrow?" I might ask.

"Tomorrow Day of Dead"

"Right, tomorrow *is the* Day of *the* Dead. What do you do to celebrate?"

The students were no longer children but they were still just as excited to practice their English and tell a stranger about their customs. "Yes. Tomorrow is the Day of the Dead. We will drink a purple drink, and make food for our dead. We eat with them."

Another day I might pass a protest in the street and then that would be a topic in class. Or whenever I saw something I wasn't sure about in my daily life I would bring it up.

"Why did I see so many goats in the market today?"

"It's Friday. Goats come on Friday."

"But why? Why are they here? Can you buy something from them?

"Yes, yes. You buy their milk. They give it you fresh and—"

Another student interrupts "And it good luck. Very healthy."

Soccer games were always a big deal. An easy way to get my students to talk was to ask them about Ecuador's national team.

"Is there a game this weekend?"

"Yes! Ecuador plays Brazil!" everyone would answer, their voices competing to tell me about the game.

"If win, we go World Cup."

"Good. If *we* win, we *will* go *to* the World Cup."

The university was secular but almost all my students were Catholic. Latacunga was heavily influenced by the Church and was socially conservative. On the city's warmest days it was almost shorts weather but exposing that much skin—male or female—was taboo. Likewise, premarital sex was something shameful, and theft often provoked vigilante justice.

The indigenous communities that surrounded the city were especially trusting, and occasionally people took advantage of that. Shortly after I arrived two men started selling fake property deeds in these villages. When they were caught, the entire community walked them into the mountains, buried them up to their necks, returned home and called the television station in Latacunga to send a crew out to the site. It was a warning.

My new city was a fascinating place; while it was the most socially conservative place I had ever lived, it was also the most politically radical.

The political apathy that was so prevalent where I had grown up on Long Island was nonexistent in Latacunga. People fought for what they believed in, and it seemed they usually won.

A few years before I arrived, the government decided to build a jail at the edge of the city in a neighborhood called *San Felipe*. As the prison walls were rising, so was local opposition. Residents began blocking roads to prevent more supplies and heavy machines from entering the construction site. The complex was nearly completed but the residents refused to lift their siege and demanded the government spend more money for education and less for incarceration. And they won. What began as a prison became one of the nation's first publically funded universities; the *Universidad Técnica de Cotopaxi* (UTC).

As I began to peel back my first impressions as an outsider, I started looking for reasons to never leave. I began volunteering at a government program designed to make street kids into school children. I also quit my job at the private university and moved across the city to the new public one in *San Felipe*.

Each day, after I finished lunch, I walked to INNFA (*Instituto Nacional del Niño y la Familia* / National Institute for Child and Family) to supervise a hundred children finishing their own midday meal. In Ecuador, children of poverty-stricken families were often forced to go into the streets to work. On the coast, child labor on banana plantations kept prices down, and according to INNFA statistics, it also helped give the nation the highest rate of child labor in Latin America. Within the city of

Latacunga, most child workers sold candy or flowers in the street. Others shined shoes or begged for change. INNFA sought to give an alternative by providing food as well as a place to play and study each afternoon for any child who regularly attended morning classes.

After lunch, the children washed their own dishes then streamed outside to play. There was a row of half-buried tires that they ran over or crawled through. Older kids hung from monkey bars or swung from the ropes of a swing set that had lost all of its swings. Most days someone would grab my hand and pull me to the basketball court. The children would drag a large rock or tire and set it apart from the metal pole of the basket on each side to form two soccer goals. The space was small, and the surface pockmarked with wide gaps, but each day fifty children ran wildly around chasing the ball and laughing. I played soccer when I could and had as much fun as anyone out there.

Other days the smaller children would surround me and yell "¡Salta! ¡Salta!—Jump! Jump!" They would use both hands to grip one of mine and when they jumped I would lift my hand and pull them even higher so four- and five-year-olds were 'jumping' above my own six-foot frame.

The next two hours were spent inside on homework and study. Thirty children crowded into classrooms with half that capacity and jockeyed for the small wooden chairs whose backs had not yet fallen off. The building was in poor shape: wide cracks on the concrete basketball court outside were paired with crumbling walls inside. When it rained, water dripped through the tin roof into scattered buckets and streaked down the walls, collecting in puddles on the uneven floors.

All the children knew I was different, but some couldn't quite grasp the concept.

"*¿Usted se va a su país ahora?*—Are you going to your country now?" one boy asked when I walked my bike out of the building, getting ready to leave for the day.

"No, I'll be back tomorrow," I said, not fully understanding the question.

"I know you'll be back tomorrow," he said, rolling his eyes, "but how long does it take you to ride your bicycle to your country?"

Another day, I was sitting on top of the monkey bars and fielding questions from two curious girls sitting next to me. "How long did it take you to learn English?"

"Well, in my country everyone speaks English, just like people speak Spanish here, so I learned it as a child, the same way you learned Spanish."

She looked confused and asked again, "Did it take you a long time to learn English?"

The second girl, who hadn't heard everything but knew we were talking about language interrupted, "Profe John, why does it sound different when you talk?"

*

I never got paid for my afternoons at INNFA, but reward takes several forms. Each day when I walked through the gates, no fewer than a dozen children would run up to me with wide smiles, yelling, "*¡Profe John! ¡Profe John!*" before giving me a hug and dragging me away. That was all I ever needed to keep coming back.

Each morning, before I went to INNFA, I taught classes at UTC—the jail-turned-public-university. ESPE was far better funded than UTC, and you noticed it right away. ESPE was located in the center of the city and near the park, where its massive mahogany doors opened up to white walls and stained glass. At UTC, which stood on the outskirts of the city where many of the roads were unpaved, a tall metal gate slid open to reveal a huge mural of Ernesto 'Che' Guevara.

My class size doubled, my paycheck halved, and books became a luxury the university could not afford—the teacher's edition books I used, just like the students' texts, were poor quality photocopies—but I believed in the school. I wanted to be a part of it. Free higher education was a relatively new concept in the nation, and I knew that putting my North American face behind the foreign language department would lend it some much needed legitimacy.

I took the job very seriously and tried to make up for my lack of experience by working hard. I spent extra time preparing for my classes, and whenever I could, I hung around more seasoned teachers to learn from their experience.

I was by far the youngest teacher at the university and related to my students in a different way than other professors. My pedagogy was also different. I tried to encourage discussion and critical thinking in all my classes and told my students to point out any errors I made. They were reluctant at first but soon took it as a challenge to try and stump the teacher. Often students came in with complex queries it seemed they'd spent a lot of time thinking about outside of class—and they always kept me on my toes.

Many of my students were training to become English teachers themselves and would stay after class for advice or help with their other classes. I never actually taught Fabiola, but she had heard about the new foreign teacher and waited for me after one of my Saturday classes.

"I'm working on my thesis now and thought maybe you could look at a few things," she said in perfect English.

Fabiola lived in a house painted purple and white directly behind the university. Her family mixed cement and the concrete blocks they sold to contractors were always drying in the front. She had spent a semester in Denmark studying English, and beyond trying to perfect her thesis, I think she wanted to return some of the hospitality she received when she was far away from home. She invited me over for lunch one day after class. I'm not sure what she told her family about me, but they were incredibly kind.

"Do you play soccer?" Diego, her boyfriend, asked me.

"I do."

"Well you should play on my team then. A new season is about to begin and we qualified for group C this year," he said.

My South American soccer career lasted one game.

Unfortunately, Lucía and I got looped into a spontaneous, alcohol fueled midnight match with some friends on a concrete court after the first game. I tore some ligaments in my ankle in a collision and it took months for everything to fully heal. The truth is that I was severely overmatched on the pitch with most Ecuadorians, with or without my injury, but I was growing increasingly interested in the national sport and went to many of Diego's games anyway, sitting with the team as a spectator.

I didn't see Fabiola with great frequency but she always remained a good friend. When she and Diego married and had their first child they asked me to be the godfather. It was an odd choice for a couple from two rural, traditional families to honor an agnostic, single foreigner with the title, but I was happy to oblige. Familial friction over my selection came to a head when during the party, a drunken relative, whom I had never met, threw his beer on me in protest.

While the beer soaked through my borrowed suit and made the night air cold, Fabiola told me, "I don't care what he or anyone else thinks. I want Angely [her daughter] to look up to you. I want her to have someone like you in her life."

Long before I was deported there were people or places that could be hostile because of where I was born, but I never really noticed it because it was drowned out by friendly people and events that pointed toward a more hopeful future.

I loved teaching at the university. Sometimes after closing the door to begin class, the students would stop talking and look up for direction, and I would just smile back at them, smile at the thought of it all. Whether at UTC or INNFA, I would take deep breaths and let the corners of my mouth rise into a smile. When I took a step back it was almost hard to believe everything that was happening, and sometimes, all I could do was smile. It was a dream: waking next to Lucía and helping INNFA and UTC grow.

In Motion

I also traveled a lot. I had a growing wanderlust that the city of Latacunga could not satisfy. I rode my bike into nearby towns, took buses on long day trips, and every ninety days I crossed a border to renew my visa. In February, when my cross-border trip coincided with a break in classes I decided to make it a longer trip and see some of Colombia. "Just promise to write and call me," Lucía told me, smiling. She had school projects to catch up on and wanted to spend more time with her son during the break, so the timing worked well for us.

For three weeks I traveled through Colombia. Much of that time was spent in a run-down port city on the Pacific coast called Buenaventura, where I learned firsthand about Colombia. Despite its location and dirty, industrial appearance, there was something I liked about the place.

The park near my hotel was only half a square block, had no trees and only a few large concrete boxes with dirt and plants. Benches were scattered around. It was basic and not all that pretty but it was still a public space where I could rest my legs and alternate between reading, writing and observing.

I was sitting there my second day in the city when a man approached me carrying a piece of plywood with holes cut out to hold and display about three dozen pairs of sunglasses.

"*¡Gafas de sol! ¡Gafas de sol!*—Sunglasses! Sunglasses! Would you like to buy some sunglasses?"

This question was directed at me, and I looked up just long enough to glance at him and say "No thank you." He sat down next to me and told me how sunny Buenaventura was and how affordable his glasses could be, but I didn't budge. Then he changed the topic and asked in a casual tone, "Where are you from?"

"New York," he repeated back to me. "Oh, it must be nice there. What are you doing around here then?" I looked at him for the first time. His skin was very dark, his stature short and his head was bald save for a few coarse white hairs that grew in a faint horseshoe pattern around the back of his sweaty skull.

"I teach English in Ecuador, but at the moment I'm on vacation. I just wanted to see Colombia, maybe go to a beach."

"An English teacher?" His face brightened, revealing a single gold tooth. "I'm studying English at a school just two blocks from here. Do you want to go see the school? They would love to meet you there."

"Sure," I said, closing my notebook.

Five minutes after walking into the small school, I met the director. I told her I had to get back to Ecuador later in the month but she was happy to hire me on a day-to-day basis, for as long as I liked. I taught my first class that evening. I used the job to discuss Colombia with locals and spent my days learning about cocaine and free trade, politics and guerilla warfare—and I got paid for it. Buenaventura is extremely isolated, as the Pacific coast is almost entirely undeveloped and lawless—it was guerilla territory.

Despite Colombia's natural beauty and friendly people, the nation was also host to tremendous violence. There were a variety of armed groups that controlled their separate fiefdoms, the general rule being whoever had the most guns won. This had been going on virtually without pause since 1948, but starting in the 1980s the cocaine trade began to heavily influence the fighting. The government and a myriad of rebel factions fought over control of territory and cocaine. War had, unfortunately, become part of life in Colombia as almost everyone alive there then had known no other time. Along with the government, the biggest player was a Marxist group, dating back to the time of Che Guevara, named FARC (*Fuerzas Armadas Revolucionario de Colombia* / Revolutionary Armed Forces of Colombia), though there were often more than a half-dozen heavily armed groups operating at any one time. Another leftist guerilla movement, the *Ejército de Liberación Nacional* (ELN), had thousands of fighters. There were also numerous right-wing militias that had risen in response to the guerillas and often worked at the behest of large landowners. At the time, prospects for peace looked dim.

In 1984 FARC entered an indefinite cease-fire with the government and many members joined a new political party called *Union Patriótica* (UP) that was formed in 1985. The new party had many of the same demands, such as land redistribution, that the guerillas had been fighting for. The UP grew quickly and in the 1986 election had the greatest showing of any leftist party in Colombian history, electing several senators and congressmen. Unfortunately, this led to an uptick of violence against UP-elected officials and party members. In the following years thousands of members were murdered by right-wing militias, including the party's leader and eight of its congressmen. In 1987, as violence spread among public figures, the ceasefire began to breakdown. After the UP presidential candidate was assassinated before the 1990 election, the party dropped out of the election and effectively collapsed.

In 2006 the fight, by then primarily between FARC and the government, was raging. It's estimated that the guerilla force had 20,000 fighters and 3,000 hostages at the time. FARC was primarily based in rural areas and along Colombia's borders. Unlike the much more developed and populated Caribbean coast, Colombia's shoreline along the Pacific was sparsely populated.

Buenaventura was a government town in rebel territory and often a flashpoint between the two forces.

Sitting in the park my second week in the city, a man sat down next to me. "I've seen you here before. What are you doing in Buenaventura?" he asked.

"I like this park. I'm just traveling, but I'm also teaching English while I'm here," I told him.

"You have to be careful," he said. "There are many guerillas in this area, and some of them don't like Americans."

"I had heard that. But there aren't any in the city, so I should be alright."

He smiled at me. "We are everywhere. We just wear civilian clothes when we come into the city." He stood and walked away before I could gather a response.

The conversation scared me a bit. I wasn't sure if it was a threat, or just helpful advice.

The next day, I took a speedboat an hour north to a small fishing village only accessible by sea. Although it rained most of the time I was there, during one break in the clouds I wandered off and stumbled upon a desolate cove on a black sand beach. Smooth black rock formed a vertical semicircle of cliffs that isolated paradise. To one side, waves crashed violently against the wall while on the other they died out in the sand within a vast cave, where water dripped down from the ceiling into small pools, disappearing into the sand. Within the cove, water trickled down the cliff in a dozen tiny waterfalls, sometimes right off bright green plants that had managed to anchor themselves into the otherwise smooth black rock. It was one of the most spectacular places I had ever laid eyes on.

The following night when I returned to Buenaventura, I found a cheap hotel and went to sleep, unsure how safe it was for me to stay in the city any longer. I went out to breakfast in the morning and noticed machine guns on every corner, snipers on rooftops and the army behind makeshift bunkers in the middle of town. That made my decision easy; I left immediately. I later learned that shortly after my departure the guerillas attacked the town; their assault failed but both sides suffered heavy losses.

*

Lucía and I traded emails while I was in Colombia. Two days before my trip ended she wrote me that we needed to talk once I returned and told me she would be in Latacunga to meet me. I knew something was wrong as soon as I saw her. She was quiet and sad. I led her into my room and closed the door, sealing us inside together.

"I'm sorry. I'm so sorry, but . . . but . . . I got married this week." Tears streaked down her face. We were sitting at the edge of my bed and she buried her head between my stomach and leg as I reflexively put my arm around her.

"What?! What are you talking about? You're not married."

"I'm so sorry, John, but I had to do it. Lenin [the father of her child] is an awful man and said he was going to take my child away. He said he would take away my baby if I didn't marry him."

I sat still, unable to move. She picked up her head, met my eyes with hers and said, "I love you." She slowly and clearly enunciated every word and her voice hung in the air long after her head fell back down into my lap.

I felt no anger or sadness, at least not at first. More than anything else I was in shock. Lucía sobbed, her head resting on my thigh, but I just sat there, frozen, unthinking.

"He raped me," she said without picking up her head.

My mind was beginning to function again but I didn't speak or move. My Spanish was much improved from a few months earlier but there were still large gaps in comprehension. Did she really just say that? Am I understanding everything correctly? I finally managed to squeak out a single word. *"¿Que?"*

"I never wanted to be with him. He was much older than me and always found excuses to talk with me."

"What?" I said again.

She sat up and turned her head slightly to look away from me and told me the long story; I didn't interrupt her again. Some words were new to me but I clearly understood the general idea and in the months to come, as fragments of the story were repeated, all the details became vivid.

Lenin was in the military and stationed near her childhood home. He led her onto the base one day, took her inside an empty hanger and raped her. She was 17.

As she told her story, anger and sadness began to overtake my numbness: anger at Lenin; and sadness for Lucía.

"I was so ashamed. My inner thighs turned purple from the bruises but I couldn't tell anyone—I've never told anyone until today. He kept coming over and bringing me gifts. He told me it was supposed to hurt the first time and since we had sex we were now obligated to at least date. So we dated for a few months and I had his baby, but I've always hated him."

I cut her off. "So why did you marry him?!"

"He said he would take my child away and never tell me where he was or how he was. He said I would never see my child again. I told him I would never touch him and never sleep in the same room—but I can't lose my baby."

Her head had fallen back into my lap. Strands of her hair had stuck to her wet cheeks. I moved my hand to her head and gently brushed her hair back. And I stayed with her.

I wanted things to be simpler than they were. He was the villain and she the victim. In a strange way I felt closer and more dedicated to Lucía than ever before.

It wasn't just about Lucía though. It was about me too. I desperately wanted to be good and looked for ways to confirm that I was doing right while burying any doubt. If necessary, I lied to myself and pretended everything was alright.

Behind the Barricades: Love and Revolution

In the first week of March 2006, with rumors of a free trade agreement with the United States on the horizon, some rural indigenous farmers held a meeting a few miles outside Latacunga. Most Ecuadorians, and especially farmers, feared they would not be able to compete with their U.S. counterparts. The term 'free trade' was misleading because the U.S. government would continue to subsidize corn and other agricultural products from their country. Farmers growing the same crops in Ecuador, however, would not receive any financial help, making them unable to compete with the influx of cheaper foreign produce.

Ecuador has a proud history of resisting foreign powers and is ever suspicious of the United States. When Spanish conquistadors approached Quito, the northern capital of the Incan Empire, the Incan General Rumiñawi led the resistance. When it became clear the war would end in Spanish victory, Rumiñawi, in a final act of defiance, ordered his army to turn Quito to ashes, destroy anything of value and kill any remaining temple virgins.

More recently, most Ecuadorians believed that the U.S. had assassinated their leftist president, Jaime Roldós, in 1981, after he took a hard line and tried to reduce U.S. influence. Officially, his helicopter crashed due to mechanical failure, though most in Ecuador believed it was tampered with. Few people in the United States have ever heard of Jaime Roldós, and among official government circles his 'assassination' is widely considered a spurious conspiracy theory. It is, however, widely known among Ecuadorians and few doubt that the U.S. was involved; in fact the assassination claim was validated by John Perkin's 2004 book, *Confessions of an Economic Hit Man.*

Though the free trade agreement was enormously unpopular with the public, the government and wealthy elite stood to gain large profits with ratification.

"Did you hear about the strike?" Kleaber asked me, while his mother prepared tea for us.

"No, what strike?" I asked.

"CONAIE may have one in a few days, maybe on Monday," he said. The Confederation of Indigenous Nationalities of Ecuador was the same organization that had spearheaded the revolt in 2000 which had overthrown that government.

"In Latacunga?" I asked.

"Yeah I think so, but maybe it will be small. There is always a strike in my country, it will be no big deal," he said.

I asked around and made it a topic in my classes but no one seemed to know for certain if there would be a strike and no one seemed very concerned either way. "There are always strikes in Ecuador," everyone told me.

No one I spoke with had any idea that we were on the verge of a full-scale national rebellion.

A *paro*, or strike, in Ecuador didn't simply mean you missed work; it meant you shut down whatever commercial activity you could. In the Andes, this invariably meant setting up blockades on the highway. Between mountain cities there were few roads, so it's very easy to shut down traffic flowing into or out of an area, which can be crippling for the targeted city. On Monday, March 13, 2006, rural farmers, some of whom had been walking for days, descended on Latacunga and completely cut it off from the rest of the world. On either side of the city, hundreds of families stood in the road and built great hills of earth and fire to stop anyone who dared try to part the human sea.

I had picked up some work at a private language school

during a break in classes at UTC and after a slow morning I walked out. I told my boss that I'd return when the strike ended.

"You can call us to find out if there are students," he said.

"I'm on strike," I told him playfully. The few people that had come in told us how hard travel was and that they wouldn't be back until the *paro* was over. My boss and I both knew that no one else would come in and they wouldn't need me until the *paro* ended. But in my own way, I felt like I was joining something bigger. I walked a few blocks to Ana's shop down the road.

The shop was small, about eight feet wide and twelve feet deep, but standing between floral arrangements or sitting beside them on one of the stools stacked in the corner, there was always room. When neighbors, friends, or even strangers stopped by we either borrowed a stool from next door, or simply allowed the conversation to flood out onto the sidewalk. Like most of my other new friends I admired Ana's zeal for life and her smile in the face of hardships worse than any I'd ever had to confront. She had become pregnant when she was seventeen and while technically married, her husband was rarely sober and had other women. Even with all that, by Latacunga standards she was a feminist.

The flower shop was her second job; she also was a full-time teacher at a primary school. Between her work, broken marriage and managing an eleven-year-old with a blood disease who was starting to rebel, she still found time for our friendship. Aside from going to concerts or doctors in Quito, she had barely left Latacunga, but she was curious and intelligent and acted as a sounding board for whatever thoughts crossed my mind.

Ana pulled out a stool for me as I walked in.

"*¿Por que no estas en clase?*—Why aren't you in class?" she asked.

I sat down. "I'm on strike," I said mockingly, smiling at her.

She put down the shears she'd been using to prune a bundle of roses and turned to me with excitement. "All the highways are blocked. I knew you wouldn't have any students."

"Yeah, the streets are deserted. I told my boss I wouldn't come back until the strike was over."

She laughed.

"Is this what it was like last year when Lucio was thrown out?" I asked.

"No, not at all; today is bigger. All the major protests against Lucio were in Quito or Cuenca."

Small, localized strikes were common all over Ecuador, but this one felt different.

"What do you think will happen now?"

We let the question linger in the air.

When night fell, the downtown streets filled with dissidents who had left the two main groups on the highway. Fearing a midnight attack, many families with young children decided it was safer to sleep on an urban sidewalk.

The next day more farmers poured in from the countryside. Smaller blockades popped up all over while others marched through the city streets and camped out in front of city hall. Protesters seized a major bridge downtown and made it their central organizing hub. Word had spread quickly to nearby areas, and blockades sprang up overnight and surrounded two more cities—Ambato and Riobamba. I called Lucía from the call center across the street after I woke up. She was in Ambato. Between us was the northern blockade of her city, the southern blockade of mine and twenty-six miles of an empty mountain highway. She was worried and I told her I'd call again that night.

As news trickled in throughout the day on Tuesday, it became clear that these barefooted farmers had struck a chord and started a real rebellion.

Wednesday morning the headlines in *El Universo* read: *Indigenous Protests Against Free Trade Agreement Intensify in the Center of the Country*, and *Blockade is Expanded to Nine Provinces*. I woke up in my rented room to the smell of fires burning in the street just a few feet from my front door. In fact, fires were burning at nearly every intersection downtown. Rumors swirled throughout the city that most of the country had joined the rebellion; and I joined it too. I filled my backpack with bread and swung by Ana's shop. I had been there late the night before, discussing the latest rumors with everyone who walked by, and before I left, Ana and I had decided that we would travel to the front lines to see it for ourselves.

The indigenous farmers who started the rebellion had mostly retreated to the highways which were now under constant attack from police, but all of downtown was filled with students and urban professionals who had more than taken their place. UTC was always one of the city's radical centers so I wasn't surprised to see groups of students wearing UTC jackets or T-shirts. I even recognized some from my classes. A few caught my eye and waved.

"Teacher! *Sabía que estarías aquí*—I knew you would be here." We spoke in Spanish.

"Hola Marco. How's it going?"

"Really Good. Did you hear they took over the university too?

"No, tell me."

"There was a big protest yesterday because the teachers and director weren't supporting the strike enough. Everyone will be part of MPD now."

MPD (*Movimiento Popular Democrático* / Popular Democratic Movement) was the country's revolutionary Marxist political party. They were one of the nation's smallest parties and concentrated their influence in universities.

Ana and I continued walking. There was no traffic, no shops were open, and thick clouds of black smoke filled the air. At the bridge, we conversed with some of the farmers.

Though I was obviously an outsider, no one hesitated to talk with me, especially with Ana at my side. When I asked people how long they would fight, most responded, without hesitation, "*hasta la muerte*—until death." Some looked me right in the eyes, some stared blankly ahead, but every one of them gave me the chilling sensation that they meant it.

Each person I spoke with, whether an old man or a young woman carrying her newborn on her back, seemed to understand their situation so simply, yet so deeply. These were people who, pushed to the margins of the global economy and standing barefoot at the edge, firmly declared they would sooner die than move any farther. After a few of these conversations I knew that they would win; and that I would do all I could to help.

"*¿Te dije por qué*—I've told you why I left my country, right?" I asked Ana.

"Yeah, of course."

"This is why I left; to be a part of this," I said, spreading my arms out to indicate the tires burning in the street and the farmers we had been talking with sitting on the curb. "The world is changing—because it has to. The corporations and capitalists destroy the environment, manufacture inequality, and instigate wars so they can make larger profits. It's not sustainable, we can't go on like this, and the people here understand that much better than the people in my country."

Ana smiled. She was always proud whenever I said that her country inspired me.

We decided to see if we could make our way to the main blockade north of the city, toward Quito. This was first blockade, the one that sparked the nationwide rebellion and would be the place most vulnerable to attack. Sitting outside the closed bus terminal, parked on the empty highway, were a few pickup trucks. They were waiting around for passengers willing to pay extra to try and find a way around the blockades. For five dollars—ten times the normal fare—we hired one to take us to Lasso, a town north of Latacunga. We drove through the countryside, over back roads and vacant stretches of dirt and rocks. When the driver let us off and picked up a new set of people to ferry back over the improvised roads, we discovered we had gone past the blockade by a number of miles.

We started walking south on the deserted highway. The road, usually filled with overcrowded buses and slow-moving trucks, was empty. The two lanes of asphalt stretched to the horizon in both directions, void of any traffic and framed by the Andes rising on either side. It felt as though we were in the middle of nowhere, yet every now and then we would pass small groups or individuals walking with backpacks and duffel bags. Sporadically, a pickup truck would rumble by, and since everyone was a hitchhiker that day, it would slow down long enough for pedestrians to hop on. Smaller blockades had popped up every few miles, so these rides never lasted more than a couple of minutes, nevertheless, they were always a welcome relief. On one occasion the truck we were traveling in stopped suddenly when the driver saw a dozen people beginning to throw stones across the road. It was a blockade in its infancy. Ana and I got out and began walking once more. I picked up the largest rock I could carry and dropped it twenty feet later on top of the emerging roadblock.

When I had first arrived in Ecuador, I was fascinated with the unfamiliar dynamics of a different culture, but with time, as I became more aware and comfortable with my surroundings, my observations began to mix with participation. I wasn't just learning about a new culture, I was helping to create it.

When Ana and I started putting rocks down, the others stopped their own work and stared. My help was something they did not expect, and they came over and welcomed us as if we were old friends.

"Hello, how are you?" One of the young men greeted us politely, as the others looked on.

"Good," I answered for the two of us. "We're trying to get to the main blockade. We want to help."

He motioned to the truck parked to the side of the road, "You can ride with us, we have space and we're just about to leave."

"Thank you so much," Ana said as she kicked a rock into the road.

And just like that we had twelve new friends, twelve allies.

We piled into the back of the large open-top commercial truck, human bodies filling the space where crops would normally go. We inched along the highway and picked up another group of people a mile or so down the road. The truck was now full, with about fifty bodies pushed up against each other in the small space. I opened my backpack and gave out bread and water to anyone who was quick enough to grab it before it disappeared. When one hungry dissident realized there was none left for me, he shared his.

Thick white hairs of stubble stood out against a face that

looked like it had spent a lifetime under the equatorial sun.

"*Tú eres estadounidense, no?*—You're from the U.S. aren't you?" he asked.

"Yes."

"But you are different." His eyes narrowed. "You are one of us."

Another middle-aged man wearing knee-high rubber boots and a mud-stained wool shirt turned to us and said, "The military is attacking the main blockade." He tore a chunk of bread from the larger piece I had given him, and before stuffing it into his mouth, added, "We need to help them."

Ana and I nodded our heads in agreement.

"Everyone is heading there now. We need to keep the highways closed," he said, trailing off as he leaned to the side to look ahead, the wind whipping his face. His words were different, but his eyes carried the same intensity and determination of the farmers I had interviewed that morning at the seized bridge in Latacunga.

We encountered more large trucks as we drove on. The oversized vehicles took up lanes in both directions, taking full advantage of the empty highway. We looked at each other over the chest-high railings that corralled us inside. I understood this would be a profound day in my life.

Suddenly the handful of trucks stopped, but there were no people on the ground. The highway was empty and ran in a straight line until it faded into the horizon. On either side of us there were grassy fields dotted with trees that sloped up toward the mountains. The valley the highway ran through was almost 10,000 feet and the line of peaks on either side rose to 15,000 feet. Just a few miles to our northeast was the grandest of them all, the snow-capped peak of Cotopaxi. The caravan hadn't stopped to fight; it stopped to picnic before battle.

Ana and I stepped out into a sea of people who had no idea who we were, except that we didn't seem to fit in. I was clearly an American[1], and this was a strike against an agreement that my native country wanted Ecuador to sign. Up to this point, no one I had spoken with had treated me with anything but kindness, honesty and camaraderie, but this was different—this was a hungry mob preparing for battle. Ana looked at the crowd, then at me and said, matter-of-factly, "We should go quickly." I think we both felt more excitement than fear, but we didn't want to take any chances and rushed through the crowd without another word, coming out onto the open road on the other side.

We walked for a half mile on the deserted highway before the caravan of striking farmers passed us. They had eaten their lunch and were continuing to the blockade. A minute later a pick-up truck, with other hitchhikers already piled in the back, slowed down and we hopped on. Our ride followed cautiously behind the rebels. When we stopped the next time, it was because we had reached our destination: the main highway blockade that had isolated Latacunga from the world for three days.

Lining both sides of the highway between us and the blockade stood hundreds of soldiers, their rifles out. They stood in neat rows almost exactly along the white line of the shoulder, leaving the road deserted and creating a pathway. The uniformed men were stiff, their bodies tense; their faces young and scared.

---

[1] Many people in Latin America take offense at the United States monopolizing the term 'American' for their citizens, arguing that everyone from the Americas is 'American.' I agree, and try to avoid the word in that context as much as possible but the English language doesn't provide a clear alternative. Spanish is much easier, it's *estadounidense*.

The cluster of farmers at the blockade was facing north, toward the capital, toward the soldiers, and toward the caravan of reinforcements we had arrived with.

All around us was farmland. To one side was a massive field of broccoli and on the other side cows munched on grass, oblivious to the looming confrontation. The military held the guns, but this was still the farmer's territory.

We stepped onto the empty road as the pickup truck that had carried us turned around and drove off. In front of us, past the military, we could see the mass of rebelling farmers clustered in the roadway. Through small breaks in the sea of people we could see the fires burning, and behind that we could barely make out the great mounds of earth that rebels had pushed onto the highway. Black smoke from burning logs and tires and the blue-gray tear gas swirled together above them and melted into the air. There was a breeze blowing toward us, and while we weren't close enough to be covered in the fog of poisonous colors, the stink of burning rubber filled our nostrils and sat on our tongues. Lingering tear gas scraped against our eyes and lungs. Ana and I each held our fist to our mouth and breathed through crumpled bandanas in our hands, but we still felt it.

The rebel reinforcements lined up in groups. To reach the main blockade they would have to pass directly through the gathered military. It looked like they were about to walk into a massacre, but nothing would stop them from moving forward.

Ana grabbed my arm and pulled me away. She didn't say a word, but she didn't have to. The situation was tense and everyone knew that things were about to explode. Ana released my arm as we rushed past the farmers and approached the gauntlet of heavily armed military. I noticed for the first time that she was wearing her black leather boots and somehow, above all the noise, I heard her heels hit the pavement. Her steps were hard and fast. We walked without speaking, the military to our right and left and a mass of rebels to our front and rear, but the road was eerily void of life where we were. Halfway through, I turned around to look at the farmer's reinforcements.

The new arrivals were still close to the trucks, slowly inching forward, waiting for everyone to group. The people closest to the police began locking their arms together. Ana and I kept our brisk pace once we left the gauntlet of olive green uniforms and high powered assault rifles. We passed through the mass of farmers who had been sleeping on the highway and stopped at the line of fire across the road.

There were not many people around us here because most of the dissidents were now massed at the northern edge of the group, where we had come from. Some children were throwing more branches onto the fire and a few elderly couples were sitting down and resting.

"*Tenemos que ir*—We have to go," Ana said.

I looked back at the mass of farmers, and looked at Ana. "But..."

"I want to stay too," Ana said. "But this is too dangerous for you. You know that."

We heard a pop and saw a cloud of tear gas rise from the area the soldiers occupied. The crowd roared, and pushed forward, into the gas. I had never seen people run into gas before; I watched, stunned by their will. Then half a dozen more pops exploded at once and the crowd pushed back, running away. The children near us ran to the fight. Most of the graying men and women stayed seated but a few slowly got up and followed the children.

"*No van a abrirla*—They won't open the highway. These

people will not lose. But we have to go, it's getting very dangerous now," Ana said, grabbing my arm a second time. "We have to go," she said again more forcefully, her face muscles tensing with her words and her eyes betraying her concern for me.

We walked to the side of the highway and onto the gravel and weeds at the shoulder, past the piles of earth and back onto the open highway.

We had spent all day traveling to the blockade and when we finally got there we didn't know what to do. Our plan to witness with our own eyes had ended once we stepped off the pickup truck and walked through the gauntlet of soldiers.

When we set off that morning neither of us knew where the blockade was, just that it was north of the city. Even when we were dropped off after our first ride we had no idea how much we had overshot it. It was actually much closer to Latacunga than either of us thought, but I'm still glad the journey took so long. Hitching on the empty highway, placing stones on the miniature blockade and traveling in the farmers' caravan all connected me to the place in a way I had never felt before. I was still young and naïve but somewhere along the abandoned highway I lost any notion that Ecuador might be temporary for me. When Ana and I hitched the last stretch back to the city, I was going home.

While I was moving south, back to Latacunga, Lucía, unbeknownst to me, was walking north. I still did not have a cell phone, and even if I did, Ecuador only had cell coverage in the city centers, so there was no service at the blockade or the 26 miles between Lucía and me. She had walked most of the day though similar blockades. She was still on the highway when Ana and I returned to Latacunga.

As soon as I reached my rented room I collapsed onto my

bed. A few minutes later I heard a knock on my door. Lucía's hair was matted down with sweat and her clothes were caked in a layer of fine dust. But she was beaming, wearing an incredible smile and a bulging backpack on her shoulder. She burst through the entryway and wrapped her arms around me before I even had a chance to speak.

"This might last a long time—and I couldn't wait to see you," she said. She had walked the last three miles alone, and through a city under siege.

There was nothing I wanted more. That day, lying exhausted on my bed with Lucía at my side, both of us reeking of sweat and fire, I decided to take a cue from the farmers and make Lucía the lopsided battle I would refuse to give up on. Lucía became a sort of personal revolution for me. She had come to represent the promise of a better tomorrow that I had become so infatuated with. We had our differences and she had lied to me about her own history when we began, but we loved each other, and if we could make it to each other that day, then why not every other one to come.

*

In the following months Lucía and I grew ever closer. Then, late in the spring of 2006 she came to my door with that same look of self-pity, and shattered my reality for the second time. We walked into my room and sat down next to each other on the bed.

"You're going to hate me," she said.

"No, I won't. You know that I love you. You know that you can tell me anything and I will still love you."

"Promise?"

"Yes, always and forever."

"I've been married the whole time. We married before my son was even born. Since the first day I met you I have been married." She paused and her tone changed from sadness to desperation. She spoke quickly. "I never believed I could change anything until I met you. You're the one I want to be with." Almost as an afterthought, she added, "I'm getting a divorce."

I didn't respond. I didn't make a noise nor move a muscle. Lucía put her head on my lap and wrapped one arm over my legs, as if she was hugging them. I just stared forward. My Spanish had improved and I was sure I understood her words correctly, but it took me a long time to react to them.

Lucía was crying in my lap and her sobs were getting louder. I realized I was crying too. I looked down and saw that my hand had moved onto her back. When Lucía sat up she looked me in the eye and held my gaze as she fell back onto the bed and lay down next to me. She put her arm out and I lay down on top of it. We held each other tight. Water continued to streak down my cheeks and Lucía sobbed on and off.

"He violated me, but I want that to be my past. I want a better future. I want to be with you."

And I still loved her. It's not easy to explain or rationalize now, but I still loved her. I still wanted to be next to her. All of my anger went to a faceless man in a military uniform, and all of my heart went to helping Lucía break from her past.

Crossing the Border with Lucía

The U.S. Embassy in Quito advises against travel to the northern border of Ecuador, to include the provinces of Sucumbíos, Orellana and Carchi and northern Esmeraldas Province. U.S. Government personnel are restricted from travel to these areas due to the spread of organized crime, drug trafficking, small arms trafficking, and incursions by various Colombian terrorist organizations. Since 1998, at least ten U.S. citizens have been kidnapped near Ecuador's border with Colombia. One U.S. citizen was murdered in January 2001 by kidnappers holding him for ransom.

—Excerpt from U.S. Department of State Profile on Ecuador (2006)

The next few months were chaotic. I had been in Ecuador a year and a half, but my former life in the United States felt a lifetime away. My life was full of conflict and intense emotions as my attachment to love, land and revolution grew and intertwined.

I was more bound to Lucía then ever. We started to fight more, usually when we were drinking. She continued to be jealous of almost any woman who spoke to me and I started to mimic the behavior. But we always woke up next to each other the next day and made ever deeper commitments to the other.

"I want to be closer to you," she told me one morning. "I don't want to live with him anymore."

"What about your son?"

"He's everything to me, but I can still see him often. I just need to get out of that house. I want to be with you."

Lucía moved to Latacunga and began renting a room that Ana and her mother found for her behind their shops.

There was so much hope in the air; it felt like the whole world was about to turn over. During the indigenous uprising of March 2006, Rafael Correa, a college professor from the nation's capital, had shouted above the noise of rubber bullets and tear gas and promised the nation all of its dreams—and we ate it up. While the revolting class in Cuenca was mostly urban and professional, the March rebellion, which began in Latacunga, was dominated by rural farmers and the indigenous. Correa was able to speak to both of these groups, and in many ways unite them. He articulated their concerns in a way that made everyone listen and made everyone believe. He would expel the U.S. military and reject the Free Trade Agreement; he would stop paying the country's debt to first-world nations; he would throw out the ruling class and rewrite the constitution; he would do no less than lead a revolution and completely overturn the existing order. Correa created a political party and declared his candidacy for president in the upcoming election, vowing a new kind of revolution in what he referred to as *la Revolución Ciudadana*—the Citizens' Revolution.

Lucía's mother, Mayra, was a well-known and active member of the small jungle city she lived in. As I absorbed Lucía's stories about Mayra, I tried to fit her into the world I had grown up in and imagined her as the outspoken president of the local parent-teacher association, with a pulse on all the neighborhood news and politics. She was a supporter of Correa long before most of the nation had even heard his name, and Correa asked her if she would like to help him campaign. She accepted and ran in the local elections alongside Correa in Succumbios, a jungle province in the northeast corner of the country.

In Ecuador the campaign season only lasts a few months, and each week as Election Day neared, Correa not only rose in the opinion polls, but his promises became ever bolder. All but one of the established political parties mocked and attacked him. He was, after all, threatening to throw out all nationally elected politicians if he won (whether he had the authority to do this was another story). The only established party to support him was MPD, the same one that had taken over my university during the March uprising. The university still functioned as a center for education, and was always a politically active one, but after the March uprising, the walls were covered in exclusively MPD propaganda and the auditorium hosted their speakers.

Toward the end of the semester I was on my way to class when the Foreign Language Department Director stopped me outside his office. He spoke to me in Spanish.

"John. Great to see you."

It wasn't great to see him. I never trusted him. He always seemed too opportunistic to me and I could never tell if he liked me or just thought it made him look good to have a foreign teacher.

"Good afternoon, Director."

A few students were walking by and he took a step closer toward me to give them space to pass behind him. He didn't ask me to step inside his office so I knew the conversation would be quick. "You've got an exam today, right?"

"Yes, I do. I think the class should do well. At least the ones who show up."

He forced a laugh. "Yes, they are a good group." He looked down the hallway; no one was coming. "There are a few in there who are doing good work for the party too. It's tough to balance that with studying sometimes, so maybe we can give them a break." He handed me an attendance sheet for my class with some of the names highlighted with yellow marker. "Everyone who is marked is doing good work, so please do make sure they get a good grade today."

I stared at him without responding. The bluntness of it surprised me. Political favoritism had become more common in the university, especially among the staff. Initially, I didn't argue but I did always ignore any political instructions I was given. Had I not been the lone foreign face in the foreign languages department I'm sure I would have been fired long ago.

Up to this point I had idealized the politics in Ecuador and only permitted myself to see the changes in wholly positive terms. It was similar to how I engaged with my romantic life. Whether it was Lucía or the turbulent politics around me I only wanted to see the good. I wanted life to be simpler than it was so I redirected anything that didn't fit that narrative.

As *la Revolución Ciudadana* gained steam, it increasingly turned nationalistic. I hated nationalism. It's what had driven me from the U.S. and the last thing I wanted was to see it rise in my new home. Besides that, as a foreigner working independently I knew nationalism could make me into a target. I hoped the trend would reverse, though, and I still blindly supported Correa and the emerging political order of his government.

I wanted the revolution around me to be my own but that was much easier to rationalize when it was just a concept rather than a reality. Only much later could I accept that what mattered to me was often vastly different from what mattered to my Ecuadorian counterparts.

*

I was planning on returning to New York to attend my sister's wedding in September, so a month before, in mid-

August, I went to the Colombian border with Lucía to renew my visa. It was a month since she had moved to Latacunga and things were as good as they had ever been since she had told me about her husband.

A brisk five-minute walk separated the two immigration offices at the border crossing. Between the two offices there are about one thousand feet and one winding river. *Río Carchi*, the river that decides nations, cut a deep gorge through the soft bedrock on its long journey to the Atlantic Ocean. Rumichaca, as this crossing is named, is the only permanent link between the two nations—and it's in the middle of nowhere. Tulcán, Ecuador, to the south, and Ipiales, Colombia, to the north, are separated by ten miles of rolling green hills. While the area boasts an elevation of nearly ten thousand feet, the mountains, while still impressive, are fairly gentle compared to other parts of the Andes.

During the day a steady stream of people cross the bridge and the traffic is roughly equal in both directions. The lines at immigration can become rather long, but that was usually due to the slothfulness of the officers rather than the volume of people passing through. Ecuadorians and Colombians vacationing in each other's nation make up the bulk of those waiting in line to get their passport stamped. The locals from the border towns, at least those who cross daily, never stop at immigration. Each nation keeps their border control set back from the river, and thus it is easy enough to walk to the side of the building and get into a taxi. If these locals are questioned they flash their national ID with their local address and while technically still illegal, the police allow it. They are just crossing for a few hours, visiting friends or family, or more likely, going shopping. Although the two towns sit just ten miles apart, the prices of the same products varied widely because of government taxes and subsidies. In Ecuador gas was about a dollar a gallon and almost twice that in Colombia, but buying a pair of jeans in Colombia might save you a third of the price.

While the two towns bustled with people and goods traversing the two-lane concrete bridge, the actual crossing was the territory of a more sinister type of person. Unfortunately, I would soon become intimate with these border creatures.

When I renewed my visa I usually went to the border and returned quickly, but this time Lucía and I planned to make a weekend of it. Our two days in Colombia passed without incident, but I ran into trouble coming back into Ecuador. I was granted an exit visa in Colombia, and then walked across the bridge into Ecuador.

The police told me that I had been issued too many visas and they would not grant me a new one. It's very possible that I could have just ended it there by sliding some money under the window, but I was new to the game and didn't yet understand that immigration enforcement in Ecuador was undergoing a revolution just like everything else around it.

Confused, Lucía and I walked back across the bridge into Colombia to try my luck there. Colombia wouldn't let me re-enter without the proper exit stamp from Ecuador. As I pleaded with the officer behind the counter, a small group formed to my side. When I left the window, half a dozen men, wearing jeans and T-shirts and with unshaven faces, approached me.

"*Quiero ir a Ecuador*—I'm trying to go to Ecuador, but they say I have reached my limit, and now—"

One of the men interrupted. "And now Colombia won't let you in because you have no exit stamp."

"That's right," I said.

"That's a tough situation. Ecuador started enforcing some new laws a few weeks ago, making it tough for foreigners like you," the first man said. "They say they're old laws, but I've been here six years and I never heard of them." He feigned sympathy. "But we can help you get your stamps. You just need a little bit of money. Everyone can be bought here—how much do you have?"

I glanced around, surprised that they were advising me to bribe the police so openly, and right next to immigration. At midday there would have been a hundred people waiting in line or standing around, but it was the end of the day and the outside waiting area, composed of polished tiles underneath a roof made of metal and clear plastic that hung fifteen feet above the ground, was mostly empty. I saw Lucía standing twenty feet away, talking to a tall, well-built Colombian police officer.

I entertained the idea briefly, but I wasn't ready to do business with smugglers, or at least not yet. "I have to talk to my girlfriend. Excuse me." I said and walked away.

I joined Lucía and her conversation already in progress. "Hello," the officer said in a friendly voice as he extended his hand in greeting. His dark olive jacket was buttoned all the way up but you could still make out his matching tie underneath. He had three rows of service medals above his left breast pocket and the bright colors immediately gave me confidence that this was someone I could trust; someone I should listen to. He suggested we step inside his office to discuss my options and see how he might be able to help. I wondered if his motivations were any different from the group of men I'd just left, but a ranking officer's uniform is a lot more convincing than the dirty clothes and faces of smugglers.

Our new police ally, Mr. Rodriguez, was the ranking officer at that late hour in the day—he was the one in charge. He led us inside the building to a well-kept corner office that looked onto the mountains in Ecuador through large, plate-glass windows. He had an expensive-looking desk that held a plaque with his name, an outdated computer, and a neat stack of folders. There were two cushioned seats in front of the desk and a larger plush chair that reclined and was tucked under the desk. A small TV sat on a table in the corner and the walls were filled with certificates and awards. Once we exchanged pleasantries and small talk, he got down to business.

"How much money do you have?"

The bluntness of it caught me off guard and my response was delayed. "About a hundred dollars," I finally said.

"That's not enough. I can get you your visa and free you of your troubles, but it won't be cheap. If you want to set foot on the other side of this glass," he said, pointing behind him, "if you want to return to Ecuador again, I need more money."

I emptied my pockets and piled all of my cash onto the table. Lucía fished into her pockets and added to the pile of crumpled bills and assorted coins. We had $133.

Mr. Rodriguez eyed the pile and said, "I still need more. Do you have an ATM card? There's a bank nearby and taxis outside."

"Yes, I have a card, "I said, "but I have already used it today and can't use it twice in the same day. My bank will reject it." I lied, knowing that I had already offered a significant bribe.

Mr. Rodriguez looked at me, as if pondering the situation, then grinned. "I think $133 will just cover it," he said as he pulled the pile toward him and counted the bills again.

He called his cousin, Eduardo, who had friends on the Ecuadorian side, and we waited. For an hour we drank coffee and traded small talk during commercial breaks of the *telenovela* that was playing on the TV.

When Eduardo finally arrived he looked like the *coyotes* (smugglers) I'd seen outside earlier which didn't instill me with confidence. But there was one key difference: his cousin was a police captain. Still in the police office, Eduardo instructed me to give him $73 and keep $60 in my pocket to hand over to Ecuadorian police when he instructed me to. He led me to the bridge while Lucía waited with Mr. Rodriguez in Colombia. Because it was nearly 10:00 p.m. and the border was about to close for the night, there was not much international traffic, but anyone who was crossing could have plainly seen me hand a passport and wad of bills over to two smiling Ecuadorian police officers halfway across the bridge. The officers casually strolled back into Ecuador, leaving Eduardo and me to wait. A few minutes later, the two trudged back to the halfway point of the bridge and returned my passport with a new exit stamp. My passport now read that I exited Ecuador without ever entering it.

"But I need an entry stamp," I said to Eduardo, confused.

"I know. Don't worry," he said. "The $60 you paid bought you the exit stamp, but the police also cleared your record. The next time you enter Ecuador you won't have any problem with your visa limit because they erased everything. It will be as if you're entering for the first time. Tomorrow morning you'll be legal in Ecuador, drinking beers with that pretty girl of yours," he said, slapping my back as if we were old friends. "Don't worry about immigration in Colombia, just go straight to Ipiales now and get some sleep. No one will stop you—and if they do you can always call me to get to my cousin so we can work something out."

Lucía and I caught a taxi back into Ipiales for some rest and an ATM, thinking all our problems had been solved with the $133 we divided between the two nations.

The next day, after getting my stamps in Colombia, I was denied entry into Ecuador a second time. I called Eduardo and told him to come back to the border and figure it out for me. He came quickly, but was not very cooperative.

"I did my job, whatever happens now is your problem," he told me flatly.

"Your job was to fix my passport. I paid you to get me back into Ecuador and they still won't let me in." I said, raising my voice.

Other smugglers, many of whom I had met the night before, came over to listen.

"You need to fix this," I said to Eduardo, pushing my passport into his hands.

"I can't help you," he said, pushing my passport back and crossing his arms.

Another *coyote* stepped in. "All you have to do is slip a $20 bill into your passport before you slide it under the window in Ecuador."

Frustrated and not sure what else I could do, I walked back over the bridge with Lucía. Less than twenty-four hours earlier I had walked away from these same *coyotes*, thinking my morals were higher than theirs, but when it came down to it and my back was against the wall, I gobbled up their advice and thanked them for their help.

Ecuador was a long lesson in my hypothetical ideals smashing against a much crueler and more complex reality, but I only ever saw that in hindsight.

Immigration into Ecuador is located two hundred feet beyond the bridge on the right side. We joined the long line and waited. I made a last second decision to try and get the stamp without a bribe, but was denied for the third time. When I protested, the heavyset officer on the other side of the glass told me he'd seen me in there earlier and would personally see that I was arrested if I tried to go through again. He pointed to a sign behind him listing all sorts of offenses and claimed that I was illegal in his country. As I walked away, I could hear him repeating his threat, "Three to five years. You will rot in jail for three to five years if I catch you in here again." Not really what I was hoping for.

I had gotten my first peek inside an Ecuadorian prison three weeks earlier. A few blocks from my house in Latacunga the police allowed you partway inside to drop off and pick up laundry that inmates or their wives washed. South American jails were interesting because they were different but also especially scary for the same reason. Ana once told me about a time she was at a party that the police broke up. They found marijuana on a few people and though Ana never smoked, drank, nor had any paraphernalia on her possession, she was rounded up with the others and sat in jail for fifteen days before being released. She was never charged, never got a phone call or lawyer, she just sat in an overcrowded prison for two weeks never knowing exactly why she was even there. Ecuadorian jails are severely overcrowded and underfunded so the guards rely on the inmates to self-police. In some prisons, cells are rented by the police so that initially everyone is left to fend for themselves in open spaces and courtyards that police do not patrol. I always pushed the thought away that I risked ending up there, but the idea hung over me. In the brief moments that broke through the veneer a wave of fear would flash through me.

By this time most of the smugglers who hung around

Rumichaca knew my story. Many of them changed money, sold coffee, or otherwise were working the border, but I soon learned that they all made their real money as *coyotes*. When I walked out of the office, one man offered to change my dollars to Colombian pesos but quickly recognized me and asked how it went. He shook his head when I told him I tried to go through without a bribe. "That's why they were so upset. A twenty will do it no problem."

I put a crisp $20 bill in my passport and waited for an officer, any officer to pass by outside. With the smuggler looking on approvingly, I stopped the next man I saw in uniform and slipped him the cash and passport. "I'll see what I can do," he said before disappearing inside.

Lucía and I sat down on the ground, leaned our backs against the building's wall and waited. Nothing. Half an hour passed and nothing. Then, we watched as the overweight officer with an attitude walked by holding my passport and made some photocopies of its first page before going back inside. He looked at me and gave a wicked smile. "Shit, this is bad," I thought. The same guy who seemed hell-bent on arresting me knows that I disregarded his threat and tried to bribe someone else. I became convinced that I was destined to enter Ecuador in handcuffs before this was all over.

Quickly, I gave Lucía a copy of my passport and told her to go to the U.S. Embassy if anything happened. I was desperate for help anyway I could get it, but was also vaguely aware that this, seeking help from the U.S. Embassy, was an example of the unequal power relations between my native country and my adopted home. I was using my inherited privilege. In the grand scheme, I opposed this power structure which made my life and wounds somehow more important than those of others, simply by place of birth, yet when pressed I also used it. And that's the power of it and an illustration of how hard it will be to dismantle. Few people will give up power or privilege voluntarily, rather they will find ways to rationalize it and, ultimately, entrench that structure by doing so. I was no different.

Lucía and I spent the next few minutes brainstorming lawyers and politicians who might be able to help if I did manage to get myself into an Ecuadorian jail that afternoon. I wrote her a note and my parents' email addresses and instructed her to send the message as an email if I was taken away. It said that everything was fine and I was looking forward to the wedding. I didn't want them to worry.

"Baby, I'll push to get the divorce faster," Lucía said. "If we were married you wouldn't have to worry anymore."

We had casually discussed this recently but never in much depth. Up until then a trip every ninety days was more an excuse to satisfy my wanderlust than a burden. My first job in Cuenca was the only one that ever offered me a visa. Both ESPE and UTC knew my status and encouraged me to continue my border crossing work-around. "We've never gotten a work visa for an independent foreign teacher before and frankly would not know where to start," they each told me. Then there was Lucía's marriage. She had already filed for divorce but was technically still married.

Next to the main immigration building was a much smaller office that sat in front of and to the left of immigration, forming what would have been a corner if not for the narrow hallway that ran between the two. We sat down against the wall in the midday sun with a view of immigration's front doors. We held each other tight, worried that it might not last. Finally, a third officer came out, gave me back my passport—minus the $20—and told me that if I ever set foot on Ecuadorian soil again, I would go straight to jail. That was the last time I ever tried to bribe border police in Ecuador.

Lucía and I gladly retreated to Colombia, but that created a different problem. After getting the entry then exit stamps from Colombia that morning, I was illegal in that nation as well. But we had no choice. We walked back into Colombia and caught a taxi into Ipiales, blending into the flow of locals who passed back and forth without stamps.

I realized by this point that Mr. Rodriguez was not an honorable man, but no one on his side of the border had yet threatened me with jail, and I took a lot of comfort in that. Plus, Colombia, in addition to cocaine trafficking and civil war, was also the kidnapping capital of the world and had the largest refugee population of any nation on Earth. Thus, Ecuador maintained strict border control, trying to keep Colombia's problems from spilling over, but there were no regular checkpoints on the Colombian side—contraband and people were leaving Colombia, not entering. It was getting late and we needed a break to clear our heads. Lucía and I decided to grab dinner, get a hotel, and try crossing again in the morning.

I was stuck in this nation-less stalemate, illegal on either side of the river, for almost a week. I walked back and forth over that same two-lane bridge close to fifty times that week, and each time was unique. I walked across with police, with Lucía, with soldiers, with smugglers, alone, thinking that I would soon be in jail, thinking that I would finally be legal, and sometimes, thinking nothing at all.

That week I earned an education in borders.

I sat playing cards or having idle conversation with the money changers and other men who worked the crossing. They would check their watches often and periodically point to an approaching truck.

"See that brown truck coming toward us?" one of them asked me.

"Yeah."

"Watch it. The police won't check it." He smiled. "That one's mine."

"What's in it?" I asked.

"Cocaine," he answered. "It all ends up in your country, but sometimes it's safer to ship it from Ecuador so we bring it across here."

"Is that the only thing you smuggle?" I asked.

"No, we can get anything across. A lot of cocaine crosses here but sometimes the trucks have guns. FARC keeps a lot of weapons in Ecuador."

FARC was especially active in the border region between Ecuador and Colombia at the time. The government controlled the official crossing but much of the nearby borderlands were rebel territory. The guerillas kept some supplies across the border within Ecuador because they felt they were safer from detection there.

As an afterthought, the smuggler added, "For the right price I can put you on one of those trucks, get you wherever you want to go."

"Yeah right, just like Eduardo. No thanks, I'll figure something out." I told him.

While I was stuck between nations, Colombia's civil war and cocaine trade moved freely between them. The theory of borders was beginning to reveal itself as the opposite of the reality. The window screen was keeping me out while making rich men of drug smugglers, arms dealers, and corrupt police.

I was so grateful to have Lucía. Having her next to me, holding her hand, made it bearable, at times even humorous. Unsure what to do or who we could trust, we went to the Ecuadorian consulate in Ipalies, Colombia and explained my situation. The first day they didn't have any answers, but we found out that the secretary was from Ambato and grew up in the same neighborhood Lucía had been living in. They became friends and the next day, the secretary introduced us to another woman. Lucía found common interests and made small talk for half an hour before she casually asked what could be done for me. Finally, after a week stuck at the border, and with Lucía working her people skills, I was granted a special transit visa from the consulate.

"I'm traveling to the United States for my sister's wedding next month. Will I be able to return?" I asked.

"Yes, your girlfriend told me about that," she said. "Things have been crazy here the last few weeks and they are making things harder for you, but this should fix everything and give you a clean record. You won't have any problems coming back."

I joked with Lucía that I would write a book about the experience and call it *Cruzando la Frontera con Lucía*—Crossing the Border with Lucía. I had no idea that my week of being stuck between nations was just the beginning, a sort of introduction to the next year of my life.

Bleeding Hearts

A few days after returning to Latacunga from my border trouble, and while preparing for my month-long trip to New York, Lucía and a few of my closest friends gathered to send me off. The day before I had let the lease on my celestial blue box expire, packed up my things and carried my duffel bag across town to Lucía's new place. When she moved she had taken an odd collection of things with her. There was a plush queen-size bed with a thick pink comforter but no frame; the mattress laid on top of flattened cardboard boxes, separating it from the cold cement floor. There was a TV at the foot of the bed and a cheap desk behind it holding her computer. A brand new, dark green couch squeezed against one wall, which along with the edge of the nearby bed formed the living room where we entertained our guests. The walls were an ugly lime green and mold grew in streaks where rainwater dripped in.

There were seven of us sitting in a circle in Lucía's room. These were the people who meant the most to me. Ana and Kleaber were there, and Veronica came with two others. Each of them gave a short speech about our friendship.

Veronica toasted, "When I met you in the park, I had no idea that you would stay. No idea that you and Lucía would be together. You're a special person and I thank God that he put us in the park together that day. I thank him that you are in my life."

Ana went next. "When Kleaber brought you by my shop that first day I thought you were a tourist, just another gringo. I never liked Americans before; I always thought they were all capitalists and imperialists with cold hearts. But you have the kindest heart that I know." She laughed. "And you're crazy. I remember how excited you were when we went to the barricades. I never thought an American could care about my country so much. You taught me that nationality doesn't matter; we are all just people who share this world. Enjoy New York but don't forget about your family here in Ecuador." We all raised our glasses.

I was on the verge of drunkenness and giddy with joy. As each person spoke and I looked around our small circle, I felt a wave of warmth pass through my body and my face stuck in a wide smile. After everyone had finished I spoke to them all.

"Everyone here is like my family. It was difficult when I first arrived but all of you helped me, all of you were kind, and now I never want to leave. This is a dream, my life is a dream here. This is everywhere I want to be, and it is because of everyone here. I miss my family in New York, but all of you have made this my home."

Lucía and I snuck away from the others for a few minutes and talked excitedly. We were both so happy to be with each other, so happy that this was real. We had been talking about moving in together for a few weeks, ever since she'd left her husband and came to live in Latacunga, but the day before we had actually done it.

We drifted into conversation with our guests, but when Lucía got up to find new music to play, I followed behind. She giggled and gave me a kiss when she turned around and saw me.

"*Hola*," I said, smiling, clasping my fingers in hers.

"*Hola mi amor.* It's so good to live together isn't it? I'm so happy, so happy that we are together," she said.

"Me too, baby. When I come back we will find something bigger, something more permanent for us."

In the corner of the party, just as the liquor was kicking in, we looked into each other's eyes, and the wave had never been so high. From its crest I could look out and see the rest of my life.

The tipsy joy didn't last long. Everyone had been drinking heavily, especially Lucía and I. That was always a bad combination. She was sitting next to a new guest; Veronica had invited him though we had never met. Lucía had her hand on his leg and was rubbing it as they chatted. Alcohol made her very affectionate and a more rational and sober me might not have been as bothered.

I saw her outside the bathroom again.

"I know it's not your intention, but it makes me uncomfortable to see you touching that stranger. Could you stop, for me, baby?"

"You don't like that, huh?" she said mockingly with a wry smile. Pushing past me before I could respond, she returned to her seat. She looked back at me and grinned as she placed her hand on the same man's leg and rubbed it up and down, now inching farther up than before.

Lucía continued to drink next to her new companion as the party wound down. When the last of my friends left I walked them outside to catch a taxi; Lucía stayed inside with her new 'friend' and one other male, neither of whom I had previously met. When I returned the three were standing in a tight semi-circle; Lucía was laughing and had her arms around each of them.

Both of them announced they would be leaving as soon as I returned and we said our goodbyes. The second one kissed Lucía on the lips as he walked out the door.

For a long time I had been burying things that upset me. Everything boiled over in that moment. Everything I had tucked away came out. When I recall that night and look down upon us standing in that room I don't recognize the person standing opposite of Lucía—and I don't want to.

Lucía ignored me and turned to the last bottle of rum.

I grabbed the glass from her hand and dropped it purposefully to the floor, watching it shatter. Then I grabbed the bottle and poured the last of the amber liquor over the shattered glass. The rum splashed up from the floor and scattered glass shards, making the air drunk with its scent.

Lucía screamed, took out her new cell phone and began dialing. "I'll find another man to sleep with tonight," she said loudly, almost at a shout.

Without hesitation, I snatched the phone from her hand and snapped it in two.

If breaking the glass had escalated the situation, this turned it downright bloody. She attacked me with the same rage I had shown an instant earlier with her phone. Neither of us seemed to have any control. She punched me in the face over and over again, pulled my hair and even bit me, anything to make me hurt. I stood in disbelief. We had fought before but never anything as intense as this, never anything physical. I didn't move or try to defend myself, and deep down, there was a part of me that liked it, that never wanted it to stop.

I let my mouth hang open, taking rapid but shallow breaths that dried out my tongue.

"You're just a whore."

She swung at me, connecting her fist with my face again.

I screamed at her, daring her to continue. "You've always been a whore. You'll always be a whore."

We both collapsed onto the bed, with our backs turned to the other, both of us sobbing. She began cutting her wrists with a broken plastic knife, letting blood drip down her arm. I grabbed it from her, jabbed it into my own veins, then tossed it aside. We were competing to inflict the most pain. My mind was blank and in that moment it just felt good to bleed.

Any distraction, even physical pain, was a better alternative than my mind processing the situation.

When she hit me again, I got up and walked outside in my socks.

Completely mindless and fairly bloody, I walked into the courtyard and then into the street. It was now three or four in the morning and the dark streets were deserted save for the odd speeding car. I lay down on the sidewalk and gazed up at the stars; and I felt peace.

Staring up into the cloudless night a single thought entered my vacant mind and woke me from my slumber: Lucía. What was Lucía doing?

I walked briskly back to her apartment and met her in the courtyard. She was on her way out.

"Where are you going?" I asked her.

"Nowhere!" she shouted.

"Where are you going?"

"I'm not telling you!"

She tried to walk around me but I stopped her. She pushed me.

"Please, just tell me where you are going," I said.

"No!" she yelled, and swung wildly into the air, trying to hit me but not watching where her fist went.

"You are not going to be alone tonight."

She looked up at me with big wet eyes.

"If you don't want to be with me, I will go with you in a taxi to Veronica's house. Even if you want to go to Lenin's house, I will get a taxi and go with you until the front door. But you are not going to be alone tonight," I told her.

She collapsed into my arms and started sobbing. When she looked up again she said, "Let's go inside."

Exhausted, we fell asleep together.

Overnight our bodies had found each other and we woke with our limbs intertwined. Broken glass, spilled liquor and dried blood surrounded us.

"I'm sorry," I said. "I don't know what happened last night."

"I'm sorry too." She kissed my forehead then pulled back and stared into my eyes. "Do you still love me?"

"Yes."

"Me too."

We lay next to each other looking into each other's eyes. I watched her eyelashes as they shut together and then opened again. "Are we going to be okay?" I asked.

"I hope so. Last night was a mistake. I'm so sorry, John." Her eyes broke from mine and her voice softened so I had to strain to hear it. She told me she was still broken from before we met, that she still needed time. "Will you stay with me?" she asked. "Will you stay with me even when I make mistakes?"

"Always."

Latacunga, with Cotopaxi in the background.

Parque Vincente Leon.

Some of my students at INNFA.

Downtown Latacunga during March 2006 uprising.

An abandoned highway blockade during March 2006 uprising.

The view from my front door.

Crossing One

October 3, 2006

Deported to the United States

During my month in the U.S. I talked with Lucía every day, and I was excited to return home to Ecuador and see her. The fight before I left coupled with my long trip out of Ecuador could have ruined us. We could have made a clean break; and maybe we should have. But she was the first woman I ever loved, and I wasn't even considering it. The fight only made me more anxious to get back so we could move on from our mistakes.

Lucía called from Latacunga full of enthusiasm a week before I was set to return, and told me, "I found an apartment near the bus station. It has a nice kitchen, and I think you would like it—I can't wait for you to see it." The next day, after riding buses through the night she was with her mother on the campaign trail and spoke with the same infectious energy. "Today we took a canoe to a village on the river. There are no roads to get there and everyone speaks Shuar [an indigenous language in the Amazon]. It's so peaceful, when you get back I'll take you there. And baby; we're going to win."

"What do you mean?" I asked.

"The election. Rafael Correa is going to win. He came with us today and there's something special about him. When we win, my mom says that we can go with her to celebrate with the new government in the capital."

"I can't wait to come home, baby," I told her.

On the plane ride down I wrote her a long love letter to pass the time, and when the flight finally landed, I saw her. Just before new arrivals go through immigration, they pass within a few feet of a food court open to the public, and there she was, smiling broadly and waving frantically, waiting for me. I slowed my walk just enough to smile and think how happy I would be to hold her in my arms. When I saw her through that glass, all I thought about was how much I loved her and how great things would be.

I rushed down the stairs and through the vast open space where lines formed for immigration, beating most of the people from my flight for a spot near the head of the line. I handed over my passport, smiled at the policewoman, and asked how her day was going. Usually, I would have had my passport back in hand by the time she'd answered, but the policewoman held on to the document, staring at her computer screen. She was a few pounds overweight with black hair tied tightly in a bun. Her cheeks were colored red with makeup and her eyebrows outlined with a thick black pencil. She seemed unsure of herself and unhappy as she punched each key and stared ahead, ignoring me and my question.

When she did look up, her face was blank and her eyes darted away from mine. In rapid fire she asked me a series of questions: How long have you been in Ecuador? What are you doing here? How did you get your visa the previous month in Colombia? The policewoman stepped away with the same empty look on her face and told me to wait; she took my passport with her.

Immigration control sat at the far end of one enormous room. The escalators that carried all the passengers down from the various gates slowly churned out their human cargo, pushing them toward the other end where they could be processed and stamped. Underneath the stairs a cluster of police sat idly, hidden in plain sight. The ceiling was at least fifty feet high, and during busier times the vast space turned into a maze of lines—but when I stood at the desk it was late, and the room was nearly empty. The failed crossing from Colombia a month earlier was still fresh in my memory and I was extremely anxious standing there alone at the abandoned counter. Still, I held out hope that it would be okay. That everything would be okay.

During my week between nations on the Colombian border, I realized that different immigration branches interpreted the same laws in different ways, and they seemingly knew nothing about how the other branches operated. I knew my visa was unusual and I assumed that was the cause of the policewoman's confusion. In the end it would be okay and I would walk through the glass doors straight ahead, and into Ecuador. At least, that's what I was hoping.

As the minutes dragged into an hour and everyone from my flight not only went through, but picked up their bags at baggage claim and left, I began to lose hope. I started to seriously consider that I might not be allowed back into Ecuador, and the thought terrified me. The single duffel bag I'd checked completed a series of loops around the baggage claim until finally someone picked it up, put it on the ground and turned off the conveyor belt. About fifty feet straight ahead, sitting on the floor with no one around, it was waiting for me. Lucía was waiting for me. Ecuador was waiting for me.

When the policewoman finally returned, she handed me my passport open to my newest stamp: *EXCLUIDO* (BANNED). Three police appeared and stood behind me in a tight semi-circle as she explained that airport immigration was not recognizing my latest visa, and as a result, I was being deported.

"No! I got the visa last month in Tulcán. You can't do this!" I yelled.

She looked down.

I went on, "Please, no. Please, I live here. I work here. Please, you can't deport me, you can't, this is my home!" Water rolled out of my eyes and dripped onto her desk. I became more desperate and gripped the desk with both my hands as the police moved in. "My girlfriend is waiting for me. I saw her in the food court waiting for me, I have to see her! I have to!" I yelled.

She never responded. She never even looked at me.

Two policemen grabbed me by the shoulders, pulled me away from the counter, and led me to the far corner of the enormous room. "What did I do wrong?" I asked them as we moved together, like one solid mass connected by the tight grip at the top of each of my arms.

Underneath the stairs a group of police formed a perimeter around my body, locking me inside.

I pushed and pleaded until, finally, they let me see Lucía. We cried on each other's shoulders and exchanged kisses and whispered plans before she had to leave.

"I will fly to Colombia and sneak across the border. Nothing else matters. I love you," I told her.

When she walked away, escorted by one police officer while a group of them stood guard around my body, I felt a void. Before a policeman led her away, Lucía gave me a sunflower. Then I watched helplessly as she faded into the sea of people.

It didn't seem real. I thought I had found direction and meaning. I thought I finally knew my place in the world, and that had filled me with hope and dedication. I wasn't conscious of it then but things were never as good as I imagined. I was never as good as I imagined. The politics, Lucía, my effort for personal revolution, all of it was flawed. But I closed my eyes to everything that didn't fit. Part of me must have known that even then, even while forcing a smile when one of our guards took a photo of Lucía and me. Still, at the time, I believed my life was a dream come true—a dream I was dangerously close to losing.

A Prisoner in the Airport

Quito's airport closed at night and my flight was among the last in that day. Though the largest in the country, the airport was rather small by North American standards, and everyone went home at night. During the day the building seemed surprisingly well kept and modern for a nation that, until recently, based its entire economy on the banana. However, once night fell and all the tourists left, there was no one to impress, and a new darker side emerged.

The place was entirely deserted; much of the electricity had been shut off, leaving the travel hub uninvitingly dark and cold. The long rows of gray metal seats that had seemed so convenient for waiting passengers became uncomfortable and frigid. The terminals, which by day took smiling people to warm destinations all over the world, at night became my prison. I was required to be on the next plane either to the country of my passport or the country I came from, depending whom you asked. In my case, it was the United States either way.

A group of security officers and police huddled around me. There was another foreigner who was not allowed into the country. He claimed to be living in Los Angeles, but I think his passport was Chinese. Since he spoke no Spanish and poor English, communication was difficult. I wasn't feeling very talkative, and while we never engaged in conversation, I felt we shared something. An hour after we were put together, we were split up.

Over the next few months, as I struggled with nations trying to control the natural flow of people, I would often cross paths with others fighting the same struggle. I suppose throughout my life I had been sitting next to people who were struggling against borders and immigration laws; I just never saw them until it happened to me. All kinds of people are captured by nations and borders and every one of them has a story to tell. I'm sure he had his.

I spent the night being escorted by guns through a closed third-world airport. Never handcuffed, I was always in the middle of a group of a half-dozen or so police. The police walked around the airport on security detail, occasionally taking breaks to rest. During these short breaks I had a chance to lie down across the uncomfortable seats and close my eyes for a few minutes before being prodded to attention to continue with more mindless walking. Throughout the night I was handed off and marched around by different groups of my captors. At the time, the gravity of the situation wasn't entirely clear to me, but the whole experience was incredibly surreal. I didn't think: I simply submitted and followed commands. When men with guns told me to walk, I walked. When they told me to stop, I stopped. When they said sit, I sat.

From the beginning, the men with guns told me that my deportation would not be at my expense, that the airlines were required to transport deportees free of charge. During the night I was constantly harassed by a local representative of Continental Airlines[2], which was both the airline I arrived on and the one I would depart upon.

The man wore a dark blue suit with a black tie and hung his airport ID on a chain around his neck. He was older than me,

---

[2] While some names have been changed to provide anonymity, this airline actually was Continental.

but only by about ten years, somewhere in his mid-thirties. His hair was short but neatly parted to the right side and when he spoke he held his hands in front of him, one hand gripping the other wrist so that the arms formed an upside down triangle from his shoulders.

"Sir, you need to pay for this flight. Please give me a credit card so that I may charge it." His Spanish was slow and clear.

"I'm not going to pay for a flight that I do not want to be on. I won't pay to be taken away from the place that I want to be, and I know that I don't have to." I looked toward the police, but they said nothing.

"Sir, please I want to make this easy for you. If you give me your credit card then I will charge the flight to it and return it to you promptly."

"No," I said, shaking my head.

After the airline representative left I confirmed with the police that I would be transported free of charge. An hour later the man in the dark blue suit returned.

"Sir, you need to allow me to charge you for this flight. Continental cannot fly you for free."

"No. I will not pay, you're wasting your time asking," I replied.

Another hour passed before the man in the dark blue suit found the wandering posse of police and prisoner again.

"This is your last chance. Will you give me a credit card now?" he asked.

"I already told you no."

His composure broke. "You think you can do whatever you want because you are an American? You think you're some sort of cowboy or rebel? You're not. You're a criminal. If you want to come to my country you need to respect the laws here. I don't need your help; we already have your information from the debit card you used to purchase your ticket for your flight last night and will use that to charge you for this flight." He turned his back and walked away.

I looked at the police, but they shrugged their shoulders in response. Although it seemed blatantly illegal, like they were just stealing from me, there wasn't much I could do. In the end, they took nearly a thousand dollars from me in this manner. The police, though they reassured me I was correct, did nothing. After the fact, I didn't want to draw attention to myself and my fugitive status, so I accepted the loss.

I was later informed that an airline can be fined for bringing in a passenger who gets deported. Perhaps this is why they were so aggressive: trying to cheat back some of the money I had cost them.

We continued our walk around the airport as dawn started to break and employees and passengers began to arrive. When we walked by a newspaper counter I glanced a headline about some FARC bombings near the border I would soon have to sneak across. Once we reached the far corner of the airport, far from other people, the police let me sit. They sat between the wall and me.

When the final boarding of my flight was called, two officers escorted me to my gate and watched me walk down the corridor. I was alone for the first time and considered running. With each step forward, each step away from Ecuador and toward the plane, I analyzed all my options. With each step I thought about how I could escape from this prison airport and the potential consequences. I thought there was a chance I could make it, that maybe I could somehow make it past the rows of police that stood between me and where I wanted to go, but then again, maybe I couldn't. In the long run, it seemed it would catch up to me and make a bad situation worse. So I went, and walked onto a plane that would take me very far from where I wanted to be.

Once I was on the flight, while the plane rose into the sky and flew away from Ecuador, I took out my notebook and scribbled in the pages:

> *Being deported is dehumanizing. To be deported is to be treated as if you are not a person; you are caged then dumped somewhere else. When you are deported it is not because you have committed a crime, it is because you are a crime. Technically a physical act, the deepest impact of deportation is psychological. Beyond all the walls and all of its guards the most profound impact is inside each of our minds— both those being deported and those who live in a society that accepts and supports the criminalization of humanity. How can a person be illegal? Countries can be cages, large open jails, sometimes keeping people in, sometimes forcing them out.*
>
> *Money flows freely across borders, but people do not. There is something wrong with the world when currency has more rights than humanity. Every day families are torn apart as honest people and their dreams crash violently into these imaginary walls. Yet borders are also a breeding ground for exploitation and greed which flow freely, along with drugs, guns, and the like. What is the real impact of borders? For whom do they exist? What do they encourage and what do they destroy?*

The Boy with the Flower

Five hours after I watched Quito disappear out the airplane window, I exited the plane at another airport—this one in Houston. Fucking Texas, of all places. On my customs form in the space to list countries visited, I wrote "none" and expected an interesting exchange when I turned it in, but to my disappointment, they didn't read it, and I walked through without a word.

I picked up my bags and felt some relief. I was in a new place where no one knew of my troubles, where I was not considered a crime. Houston was the turning point of my journey: rather than being pushed away, I would now begin to move closer to *mi amor*. I was once more in control. Holding in my hand the sunflower Lucía had given me the night before, I was strangely confident and energetic. I checked the Continental departures board, but there wasn't a flight to Colombia until that evening. I left to see if another airline had an earlier or cheaper flight, and quickly discovered that only one other airline, Delta, at nearly the exact opposite end of the airport, flew to Colombia. While the other flight was less expensive, it wasn't scheduled to arrive until the following day. Filled with urgency, I went back to Continental to buy my ticket. I probably should have long given up on that airline, but the only thing that mattered to me was getting to Colombia as quickly as possible. I expected everything to go smoothly, but it just wasn't my day.

Continental claimed it was against Colombian law for passengers to enter the country using one-way tickets. They claimed I would be stopped by customs in Colombia (and probably Continental would be fined). I did not doubt this regulation, but I knew these types of laws were rarely, if ever, enforced. With no other option, I decided I would buy the roundtrip ticket and worry about the rest later. I had given almost all my cash to Lucía back in Quito because she was broke and we were unsure when we would see each other again. Thus I was dependent on my debit card. I handed it over to the bronze-skinned Continental ticket agent, smiling smugly in his neatly buttoned navy blue suit jacket.

"Your card is not going through; I'm going to try again."

"Sure."

"I'm sorry sir, but I cannot make the purchase with this card. Perhaps you have another one you would like me to try?"

"Can you try again?"

"I can try one more time," he said, as his smile became as forced as his combed-back hair, held rigid with excessive amounts of gel.

"No sir, it's still not working. Do you have another card I could try?" He handed me the card.

"No, but this should work. Please try one last time," I said, pushing the card back at him, all of sudden feeling the drag of the sleepless night I spent in Ecuador.

The agent was clearly not pleased, but he took the card and tried once more. "Sir, you do not have the necessary funds in this account. I'm sorry but I cannot help you." Before he was even done speaking, he waved the next customer to his desk. He was looking past me and his neat smugness had returned.

At the time, I didn't know how much this same airline had stolen from me the night before, but now assumed it was enough to put my balance below the $900 ticket I was attempting to buy.

After my failure at Continental, I would have been more than happy to take the Delta flight to Miami that night and continue onto Colombia the next day, but was unsure if my scarce funds or the necessity for a roundtrip ticket would prevent this. I waited on a short line and tried to purchase a one-way ticket.

Most people go to an airport to quickly leave it, remaining anonymous the entire time. I had spent the better part of my day at two small parts of a very large airport, all the while carrying a large duffel bag in one hand and a sunflower in the other. The employees at Delta must have begun to recognize me and were intrigued to discover my story. The first ticket agent I spoke with was a middle-aged woman, with a youthful look and a constant smile. Her natural blond hair was pulled back into a ponytail. I read the name off the nametag fasted to her blouse: Lisa. When I approached the counter, there were only two other agents: two brunette women casually helping the other passengers who came by in the off-peak hour.

"You've been here all day, haven't you?" Lisa asked.

"Yeah."

"We noticed you and have been trying to figure out what happened. You look exhausted, is everything alright?" she asked.

"Yeah, I'm fine. I'm just trying to get back to Ecuador."

"But this flight is to Colombia."

"Right. It's a long story."

Lisa didn't press for details. She smiled and turned to her computer screen. Her smile melted into concentration then a cringe as she handed me back my card. "I'm so sorry but your card was rejected. I tried it three times." She pointed behind me and continued, "There's an ATM right there; maybe you can pay with cash?"

The ATM rejected my first attempt but spit out $300 when I lowered the amount. I tried other machines and smaller amounts but could never withdraw any additional money nor check my balance. I was happy to have some cash but also beginning to feel desperate when I returned to Lisa.

"Did it work?" she asked cheerfully.

"No. Is there anything else I can do? I need to get on that flight," I said, with more energy than the minimal responses I gave during our first interaction.

"Oh dear, we will certainly try. Do you have someone waiting for you down there?"

I smiled and placed the sunflower between us on the counter.

"Yes, the girl who gave me this flower."

The two brunette women, who had been discreetly eavesdropping, gushed and came over. Business was slow and whenever they were free they moseyed over to learn my story. Word spread through whispered conversations to the other staff members who were starting a new shift or had been in the back. They all eventually came over to listen in and get a closer look.

I learned a bit of their story—Lisa had moved back to Houston while her divorce in California was being finalized—and told them mine.

I told the mostly middle-aged women how I loved my teaching job at the public university, and how there was an infectious optimism in the Andean air. I told them how friendly the people were and how the elevation, coupled with the proximity to the equator, created a sense of permanent spring. But all they ever asked about was the girl who gave me the flower.

"Your eyes sparkle whenever you say her name," one of the agents told me.

"Lucía," I said aloud and smiled.

Everyone who heard my story became an ally, and soon it seemed as if everyone in that small corner of the airport was rooting for 'the boy with the flower'—a moniker the staff had christened me with when I returned, before they even heard the story. Their support gave me a sorely needed boost and new energy. The sunflower was a constant topic of conversation. In a mostly emotional and internal battle, the sunflower became a physical representation of the struggle that everyone could grasp and see and understand. From the moment the police allowed Lucía to see me, I carried hope and love with me everywhere I went; I carried it in my hand in the shape of a flower.

Running Barefoot in Houston Airport

I had not eaten or slept in nearly two days and had been through many setbacks and much heartache. At first glance I must have appeared desperate, my voice was dull and my words few, but through the wide open eyes of my exhausted body anyone could see I was on a mission. I think many of the people I dealt with bent the rules for me out of compassion. Emotionally drained, I was stuck between my two worlds without any way of leaving, and the hardest, most dangerous part of my journey was still to come. Ever since I had gotten my passport back with my newest stamp, I had almost no critical thought process. There was a mechanical quality to it and little deliberate mental debate; I knew I was on my way home but beyond that my subconscious had taken over. I loved Lucía in the deepest way I had ever known: there was nothing I would not do for her, nothing that could ruin her for me.

I threw myself at my new friends at Delta, and thankfully, they caught me. I had to get on that flight but lacked the necessary funds. Since there weren't many customers the majority of the staff was now working to solve my dilemma. One woman gave me a cup of water to put the sunflower in, and everyone else tried to get me back to the girl who gave it to me. They were calling my bank, brainstorming ideas, and recruiting others to help.

After many revisions, our final plan was to reserve a ticket in my name to be paid for over the phone with a credit card by a third party. I could turn to my parents for help, but did not have their phone numbers with me.

I bought a $20 IDT phone card from a vending machine—

the first of many I would buy—and called a friend in New York whose number I had memorized and who I envisioned to be sitting at his desk in front of a computer at the time.

He was surprised to hear from me. His greeting was joyful, almost excited.

"John, what's up man? Are you in Ecuador?"

In a tone that must have conveyed as much as my words, I said, "Actually I'm in Houston. I got deported and now I need your help."

In one breath I had summed everything up and by the tone of his voice I could tell he understood.

"Shit man, what do you need?"

"Are you at your computer?"

"Yeah."

After a short time he was able to search for and find what I needed: my parents' work phone numbers from my email account. I quickly told him what had happened and we hung up.

My parents have always supported me, but I know my lifestyle can sometimes cause them significant stress and loss of sleep. If they'd known their son was sneaking across heavily militarized South American borders and risking life and liberty in the process, I am quite sure they'd have spent their time in dread, so I carefully choreographed the conversation and de-emphasized the trouble.

"Hello, John Dennehy speaking."

"Hey Dad."

He was obviously happy to hear from me.

"Hi John. How are you? Are you in Ecuador?"

I waited a second.

"Not yet. I'm in Houston." I tried to sound optimistic and cheery.

"In Houston? Was your flight delayed?" He asked, assuming I never got off the ground after a layover on the way down.

"Well no, I was in Ecuador last night, but I had some trouble with my passport so they sent me back. And, actually, I'm calling because I need to ask you a favor."

"What do you need?"

My dad definitely sounded concerned, but he thinks clearly under pressure and handled it well. He said he would call the number I provided, purchase the reserved ticket, and then call me back at the pay phone to confirm.

I sat on the floor nearby and waited restlessly. A woman got into a long conversation on the phone he was slated to call, so I bought another phone card and called him back from a different number. He told me the process had all been automated, but he believed it was a success.

I returned to my friends at the ticket counter, desperate to move on from this ordeal, but not overly optimistic as the roundtrip requirement hung over my head. Lisa was helping me and there were a handful of other airline employees standing close by. They checked on the computers. It didn't go through. I didn't say anything.

Lisa tried again, and on the second attempt it worked. Then she told me what I already knew: there was a problem; she could not sell me just a one-way ticket.

"Is there something I can do? How can I get on that plane?" I asked.

"Give us a few minutes and we will figure something out," Lisa said, smiling. Another woman briskly walked into the office behind the ticket counter to consult with a supervisor, and she came back with good news. She handed me a piece of what felt like fax paper. It had the airline's watermark and looked official.

"This is a false itinerary for a return flight. Colombian immigration will probably not ask you for proof, but if they do, this should work."

They were putting themselves and their jobs at risk to help a stranger in need. I was physically and emotionally numb and accepted the paper with little emotion as I flatly repeated the phrase "Thank you."

I regret not expressing deeper gratitude at the time. All along my journey, through the good times and the bad, there were incredible people that propped me up and showed me what courage and compassion could look like. I am forever in their debt. The story of my deportation and what followed is one that still makes me sad, even a decade later. But it's also a story that gives me incredible hope and inspiration.

I may have been numb, but I was as determined and focused as ever. In my mind, I knew I would get back and what happened in between did not matter, they were just details. I was saving all my joy for the next time I touched Lucía.

I had minimal time to catch my plane because of all the delays. I quickly called my dad for the last time to tell him everything was okay and ran to my already boarding flight. After I passed through security, to save time, I kept my shoes off and continued running—now barefoot—to my gate. The plane was boarding, but it wasn't leaving just yet, so I got on the internet at a nearby computer with a coin slot. Lucía had written me:

> *mi amor yo ahorita escribí mucho mucho para ti y estaba nerviosa y se borró todo, quiero llorar, yo te amo con todas mis fuerzas, yo voy a hacer todo lo que esté posible y lo que no sea posible yo lo haré por ti, mi amor espero que todo salga bien, yo voy a pedir a dios que te cuide y te proteja y voy a pedir a dios que nos deje estar juntos porque el amor que los dos tenemos es sincero, y así tu seas del norte y yo del sur tenemos*

que estar juntos porque el amor no entiende de distancias, mi vida si pasa algo en colombia solo me llamas o me dices que necesitas y yo voy hacer todo, si pasa algo yo te voy a ayudar mi vida.

Mi amor pero si no puedes venir a ecuador yo voy a presentarme para sacar una visa para ir a verte en tu país. Yo estoy segura que yo puedo esperar por ti toda mi vida mi amor, porque tu eres el motor de mi corazón y sin ti mi corazón no quiere funcionar, te amo y nadie nos va a separar ni la distancia de los países, ni migración, ni embajadas, nada porque el mundo no es de ellos el mundo es de todos, y el amor es libre, y mi amor es tuyo.

I LOVE SO SO SO MUCH mi wishes yo voy ahorita a la universidad y voy a retirar el celular para que me llames es muy necesario ahora mi amor, y espero tu estés bien mi vida yo estoy pensando mucho en ti y tengo pena porque no sé cómo estás.

te adoro cuidate mucho mi amor y espero todo salga bien pero mi amor no quiero que hagas algo que puede llevarte a la cárcel (prisión) no quiero eso mi amor, si algo no es posible hacer me dices y yo voy a presentarme para una visa para ir a tu país, pero si no resulta nada de eso, yo esperaré por ti toda mi vida, de verdad te amo, te amo, esto que siento por ti es más fuerte de lo que imaginas.

He arreglado mi celular para que me llame, es el mismo número. Te amo.

Below is a translation of her email.

Mi amor, I just wrote you so much but I was nervous and everything got erased. I want to cry. I love you with all that I have and I will do everything that is possible, and everything that isn't, for you. *Mi amor*, I hope everything ends up okay, I am going to ask God to protect you, I'm going to ask God to let us be together because the love that we have is sincere. Even though you are from the north and I am from the south we have to be together because love doesn't understand distance. *Mi vida*, if anything happens to you in Colombia all you have to do is call me, or just tell me what you need, and I will do it all. *Mi vida*, if anything happens I will help you, *mi vida*.

Mi amor if you cannot come to Ecuador I will present myself to get a visa and come see you in your country. I can wait for you all my life *mi amor*, because you are the motor of my heart and without you my heart doesn't want to work, I love you and nothing will keep us apart, not the distance of nations, nor immigration, nor embassies, nothing because the world is not theirs, the world is everyone's and love is free and my love is yours.

I LOVE SO SO SO MUCH *mi wishes*.[3] I am going to the university now to get my cell phone so you can call me if you need to. I hope you are doing okay *mi amor* I am thinking of you a lot and I feel pain because I don't know how you are.

I adore you, take care of yourself *mi amor*, I hope everything works out but, *mi amor* I don't want you to do anything that will put you in jail, I don't want that *mi amor*. If something isn't possible just tell me and I will present myself to get a visa for your country and if that doesn't work, I will wait for you all my life. It's the truth that I love you, I love you, what I feel for you is stronger than you can imagine.

I fixed my cell phone so you can call me, it's the same number. I love you.

I desperately wanted to call her, so I went to the desk now announcing final boarding, and asked if I could make a quick phone call. These were some of the same people who helped me before, so they knew my story and nodded happily. "We'll make sure the plane doesn't leave without you," one said. Still barefoot, I ran off to buy yet another phone card. The card didn't work, and I was out of time, so I got on the plane.

Two hours later we landed in Miami. The airport was nearly

---

[3] "Wishes" was a nickname she had for me.

empty. I bought a new phone card and this time got through to Lucía. It was so good to hear her voice; it felt as if she was there with me. I updated her on what had happened and what I planned to do next.

"I'll come to Colombia. We can cross together," she said.

I thought for a second, considering the option before responding.

"No, it's better if I go alone."

"Then Tulcán, I'll meet you in Tulcán."

I smiled at the thought of her waiting for me just across the border. I could almost feel her warmth slipping through the phone.

I located a board listing nearby hotels and got a shuttle to the cheapest one. The driver was Cuban and once I entered the shuttle my brief time speaking English on this voyage was over. At my hotel, I put the sunflower in water and passed out on the bed.

In the morning, I caught another shuttle and made my way to the airport. I checked in, and while waiting on the long line to pass through security, I realized I had been traveling with some banned items but no one had noticed. A few weeks earlier, British police had uncovered a plot to blow up U.S.-bound flights using small amounts of a clear liquid explosive carried in vials, and since then, all liquids were banned from carry-on luggage. Not only was I transporting small discreet vials of clear liquid this whole time, but I was doing so while sneaking into a country and with forged airline tickets. The liquids were a souvenir from my sister's wedding the week before, and although they were meant to be used for blowing bubbles, they definitely looked suspicious.

I didn't want to lose this souvenir, so I returned it to my

backpack and walked through a row of police and metal detectors for the fourth time since I left New York and the second time since I was deported and traveling with forged documents. We build walls of security for peace of mind, not necessarily because they are effective at stopping what we judge to be bad and allowing what we judge to be good.

I walked through security without a problem and put the still vibrant sunflower in the seat-back in front of me and flew back to South America.

Colombia

The Department of State warns U.S. citizens of the dangers of travel to Colombia. Violence by narcoterrorist groups and other criminal elements continues to affect all parts of the country, urban and rural, including border areas. Citizens of the United States and other countries continue to be victims of threats, kidnappings, and other criminal acts.

At least five Americans were kidnapped in 2004, and at least one in 2005. Terrorist groups such as the Revolutionary Armed Forces of Colombia (FARC) and the National Liberation Army (ELN), and other criminal organizations, continue to kidnap civilians for ransom or as political bargaining chips. The FARC have held three American official contractors hostage since February 2003. Although the U.S. government places the highest priority on the safe recovery of kidnapped Americans, it is U.S. policy not to make concessions to or strike deals with kidnappers. Consequently, the U.S. government's ability to assist kidnapping victims is limited.

—Excerpt from U.S. Department of State Travel Warning for Colombia (2006)

Two days after Ecuador vomited me back to the US, I got a new stamp in my passport: a sixty-day tourist visa at the Bogotá airport. I was hoping for ninety days, but I didn't care. All I wanted was to get back to Ecuador, and fast. While my passport claimed that I was in Colombia, I would be living in Ecuador. Truthfully, I had no idea what would happen if I didn't make it back within those sixty days, but I imagined it to be bad, the kind of bad that is worth going through a lot of trouble to avoid. Borders are fairly straightforward for a visitor, but vastly more complicated when you immigrate through them. The complexity and confusion is amplified many times more when you attempt to pass through them after you have been banned from the place. I didn't merely want to sneak in and exist under the radar—I wanted to live there; I wanted to help shape the nation, not hide from it.

I checked the domestic flight board at the Bogotá airport, changed my money and bought a ticket on the next thing flying to Pasto—the closest airport to Ecuador. I called Lucía to tell her the good news and we made arrangements to meet in Tulcán.

A few hours later I landed at a remote single runway airport north of Pasto in the Colombian Andes, squeezed into a shared taxi with others from my flight, and set off for the border. Along the way an accident shut down the two-lane artery of the Andes and stopped us dead in our tracks for an hour or so. I had been stranded several times before on remote sections of the Pan-American highway as it curves dangerously through one of the most spectacular mountain ranges in the world—these experiences never cease to amaze me. There is a unique serenity to be stuck at the top of the world, in the middle of nowhere but with dozens of others. Standing at the edge of a great cliff with only soaring mountains and no signs of civilization as far as the landscape spreads is not the same when seen through a bus window, and to turn around and see dozens of cars, engines off, occupants pacing, against this backdrop is something that will never seem dull. Amidst the euphoria, I nearly forgot the danger ahead. The accident was eventually cleared—by people, not machines, pushing and pulling the wreckage—and our beautiful interruption ended.

The taxi ride took two hours and it was dark by the time I arrived at the border. As we approached and I continued thinking of the best way to cross, I decided I would just stay in the car and get out in Ecuador as if I were a border town resident returning from a shopping trip. My driver that day—from Pasto—was unaware of this custom and stopped the car in the parking lot next to Colombian immigration. The three other passengers, also apparently unaware of the custom, exited without a word. I figured it best to blend in as much as possible, so I exited the vehicle with the others.

The isolated crossing was nearly empty and there were more police standing at either end of the bridge than there were people moving between them. The border closes at 10:00 p.m. but a few hours before that, the traffic slows to a trickle. It was about 8:00 p.m. I was nervous, afraid that if I were caught again it wouldn't be so easy to escape spending time in a South American jail.

Both love and self-preservation can make ordinary people do extraordinary things. I had seen with my own eyes how powerful the human spirit can be. In March, I had watched a handful of peasant farmers bring a nation to its knees with their uncompromising conviction.

I had never been as caught up in anything as I was with my own life then, not even close. In love with a woman and a life, no border or police force would stop me from returning to that.

No, Officer, I Don't Have Any Cocaine

When I finally arrived at the border, two days after I was deported, no one suspected that I was illegal and sneaking across. All I had to do was play the part of the stupid tourist everyone believed me to be. My bluff was walking through a sea of police and forgetting that if any one of them saw my passport and realized what I was doing, they probably would arrest me and drive me to the nearest jail—and I wasn't in a prison sort of mood that night.

I was still learning, though. When crossing into Ecuador, the immigration office as well as the massive police presence is on the right. To the left is the parking lot with taxis waiting to take you away. I now realize that I never should have tried crossing at night nor done anything even slightly abnormal, but stupidly, I walked quickly across the bridge on the left side with my head down, taking extra-long strides to get me across faster. A policeman noticed, called me over and asked me to come with him. He led me to a small empty building with a single bare room, save for an old wooden table. A lone light bulb hung from a wire in the middle of the ceiling and provided an agonizing and tense lighting.

My escort was a narcotics officer that had picked me out to search my bag and person for drugs. He was shorter than me, though muscular and bulky. His shirt was tight against his chest and he was all business. I was scared, but learning quickly. My stupid tourist act was in full swing; I played the stereotype to a T and did exactly what he expected me to do each step of the way. I pretended my Spanish was horrible, but I was eager to cooperate in any way that I could.

He motioned for me to place my bag on the table. I complied and took a step back while he unzipped it and began slowly removing my belongings. He ran his stubby fingers over each item as he placed it on the table while keeping a watchful eye on me. I had nothing to hide in my bag, but the seconds still dragged as I cursed myself for walking too fast on the wrong side of the bridge. I tried to look casual and act uncaring. He found nothing, but when he looked up and met my eyes, he asked the question I had been dreading and preparing for while he thumbed through my clothes:

"And your passport?"

My mind raced, formulating intricate lies to tell in a language I was pretending not to know, a language I was hiding behind. Still keeping up appearances and playing the role he expected me to, I looked right into his eyes with the most ignorant and innocent look I could muster as my insides turned. He flipped through the pages in one fluid motion, as if he'd done this a thousand times before. The pages zoomed past—including my deportation stamp in the middle—and he stopped on the final page. There he found the visa from the Ecuadorian consulate in Colombia that I had gotten a few weeks before. It was a full page and since it was uncommon for the consulate to issue visas, it caught his attention. He stared, confused for a second, then gave me back my passport and reminded me to get my stamp at immigration.

I'm sure if I showed how apprehensive I was, if I had let what I felt inside bleed out, his confusion would not have turned to the lazy assumption that everything was in order. Safe for the moment, it was not yet over. Though the police were no longer suspicious, there was nothing else to hold their attention, so they watched me as I walked away. I felt the bored looks of a dozen eyes on my back. I had to go to immigration or it would raise a red flag, but I knew while I could perhaps fool the people, their computers would catch me. Worse, some officers inside had threatened to arrest me just a few weeks earlier.

Thinking quickly as I walked the short distance to immigration, not able to enter yet not able to pass, I stopped and sat down. I sat on the ground and leaned against the wall of the immigration building, the same wall I had my back against a month earlier with Lucía. I took out my notebook and started mindlessly writing. Ecuadorians are always amazed how "all the *gringos* are always writing in their notebooks" so this action was hardly strange to the on-looking police. Between freedom and incarceration; a few feet in front of me was the entrance to immigration, to the left was a hallway that led toward the parking lot with waiting taxis. I kept writing until all the eyes wandered to something new, then quickly and silently made my way toward the hallway, past immigration and into a taxi.

I met Lucía in Tulcán at a hotel across from the bus station, and nothing else mattered—I was home.

Crossing Two

November 17, 2006

Home, again

Upon returning to Latacunga, I squeezed my body and duffel bag into the small drafty room that Lucía had begun renting a few months earlier. Within a couple of weeks we found a great new apartment together. A bedroom, bathroom, living room and even a nice kitchen just for the two of us right in the center of the city. At $110 a month, it more than doubled what I had been spending on rent, but it was worth every penny. I was happy. We were happy. Our landlord, who lived downstairs, assumed we were married because the local culture was socially conservative and it would be unthinkable for us to be sharing a bed otherwise. Every morning when we crossed paths on the stairs, he would ask how my wife was, and I would smile at the thought of it.

By now I had a wide circle of friends and couldn't walk for long without stopping for conversation or spontaneous activity. On my way out to the market I ran into a former student and chatted for a few minutes. Just as he left, I saw Ana walking down the block so I waited for her. I hadn't even made it off my front step.

"Have you been to *La Mama Negra*?" she asked me.

"Of course I have," I told her, surprised that she would even ask. "I'm pretty sure we hung out there together for a bit early on last year?" *La Mama Negra* (the black mother) is a celebration of the city's founding and continued existence; a prayer asking the volcano gods to spare the city in the next year. I'm not sure who decided that the volcano gods want a wild, drunken parade every year, but it's become one of the nation's most spectacular parties; everyone knew *La Mama Negra*.

"No, not that. That's just the finale. The real *Mama Negra*,"

Ana said, shaking her head and giving me a smile. Ana was proud to be from Latacunga and never tired of explaining its idiosyncrasies to me.

"There is a ceremony to begin this year's celebration right now. The parade is just a party for the city, but there's a lot more to the story. Come on and I'll show you."

Lucía was studying with Veronica and I decided I needed a break from unpacking the last of our things, so I went.

We walked to a hill overlooking the city; there were hundreds of costumed people dancing to the sound of a brass band with a very loud horn section. "All the people on the right were characters in the parade last year, all the people on the left will be in this year's parade," Ana explained over the noise. "Legend says that *la Mama Negra* was a black woman who prayed to the virgin during the last eruption, and the lava flowed around her. The highest honor of all is to paint your face black and dress up as a woman, but everyone else here represents something that is part of the story."

I nodded. I had heard this all before, though I was still a bit perplexed. Latacunga was generally a hostile place to homosexuality and cross-dressing; though it was also a place full of contrasts I never fully understood. I pointed out the irony during my first *Mama Negra* but none of my local friends ever thought it strange—it was like the ice cream garbage truck all over again.

"What are those? And what's he doing?" I asked, pointing to a group dressed as giant birds pecking randomly into the crowd and a man walking around and sharing a bottle of liquor.

"That bird was common in Latacunga a hundred years ago, but it's extinct now. The men with the square hats are supposed to be Spanish soldiers; they help get everyone drunk." Ana smiled as a new thought hit her. "Hey, did you know that the municipal building was made from pumice?"

"No."

"After the last eruption everything was destroyed and when they rebuilt the city they used pumice [a rock formed from cooled lava] as bricks. The municipal building here is the only one in the world made entirely from a volcano." Her eyes were grinning.

"From destruction, creation," I said.

Ana smiled and patted me on the back before launching into the rest of the characters.

After Ana taught me about the past, I came home and heard the sound of a new nation echoing off the sidewalks. "Get the rats out of congress," demonstrators chanted as they streamed by our front door. Rafael Correa had won the election and would soon be inaugurated, but *la Revolución Ciudadana* was not waiting for a ceremony. There were countless marches in the streets in support of the president-elect and his ideas. This new army had already started collecting signatures for a vote on rewriting the constitution, and there was no stopping the train of momentum that had been building for years. Given that Correa vowed to dissolve Congress, nearly every traditional politician had become his sworn enemy. With almost no political support, it was becoming obvious how he would push through his reforms: on the street. Change would still be forced from the bottom up, but now different sectors of the movement would be united in the most unlikely of places—the presidential palace.

True to her word, Lucía took me to visit Correa. Her mother, Mayra, knew I had aspirations to be a journalist and set up an interview for me. I got dressed up, and even bought a nice shiny pair of shoes before we took a bus to the capital at dawn.

A cluster of reporters was setting up on the sidewalk in front of the office tower that was serving as Correa's temporary headquarters. Inside the lobby one of the aides to the president-elect told us, "Mr. Correa will be traveling to Bolivia shortly and any appointments he had for the day will need to be rescheduled."

Lucía lied. "But we have come all the way from Lago Agrio. My mother is Mayra Acros, and she is a friend of the president. She was the candidate for Alianza Pais (Correa's new political party) in *Sucumbíos*. She made this appointment for us."

"Wait one moment, please."

When the aide returned a few minutes later he told us that the president-elect was on a tight schedule due to an unexpected trip. He would take some questions from the media on his way out though and would like to reserve the first question for me.

I didn't think I could sell an interview of a single question so I declined but Lucía and I stuck around anyway. We had come all this way and I at least wanted to see him, so we joined the group of reporters outside.

Forty-five minutes later he walked out. The reporters all immediately perked up and competed to shout questions at the president-elect. Lucía and I were close to the door and amid the initial bustle Correa walked swiftly toward us. He must have recognized Lucía from the campaign; he smiled and nodded his head to her, then he turned to me and shook my hand as he said "Nice to meet you," in English.

While I never did get a private audience with Correa, he did have an appointment with me. I don't imagine that leaders of nations meet with fugitives of their borders very often, as this was shortly *after* I snuck into the country.

*

While the revolution surged forward, I began to fall behind.

Due to my deportation, I lost my job at the university for at least that semester. I also had an Ecuadorian bank account with a small amount of money in it before I was deported, though the police in the airport told me the government would close the account and freeze anything inside. I might be able to contest it, they said, and get everything back. I had already resolved to sneak back in though, and knew that meant I would have to accept the loss without protest. I don't recall exactly how much was in the account, perhaps less than $200, but its loss plus my desire to not have any record of my presence in Ecuador meant I could only use cash. The much bigger cost was the airline charging me for my own deportation and the subsequent trip back in. Within a few short, sleepless days, I went from having a secure and highly paid job with a few thousand in savings to being unemployed and nearly broke.

Since Lucía was still in school and not working, I took on her expenses as well. Ana let me sell flowers on busy days to make a few extra dollars, and Kleaber helped me connect with students who needed private tutors. But that wasn't enough. I was also forced to trade a few of my INNFA hours for private teaching jobs I didn't like, and eventually had to stop volunteering all together—but I told myself that it was only temporary. The nation's power dynamics were dramatically shifting and I was at the forefront of the change, pushing free education forward and shaking hands with the president; and every morning I woke up next to the woman that I loved.

Lucía and I decided to make a long trip together during the upcoming Christmas break. We would travel ten hours by bus going north and east to the edge of the Amazon where her family lived. We were both nervous but excited. I would meet her whole family that week, but first I would leave Ecuador and visit mine.

My sixty-day visa in Colombia was coming to an end and I needed to return there so I could officially leave. Since I still was not allowed in Ecuador, leaving Colombia would require me to fly out. I planned go to New York to spend Thanksgiving with my family and then return to Colombia and get a new visa.

*

I was sneaking across the border again.

In both Ecuador and Colombia, immigration policies are confusing and always evolving. This inevitably makes the process more complicated because two official sources will tell you different things in the same day. For me though, all that mattered was that I had been banned from Ecuador for the remainder of the year and my visa was about to run out in Colombia. Still learning as I went, my plan was to cross back into Colombia in order to fly to New York. When I returned to Colombia the following week, I would obtain a new visa and then sneak back into Ecuador. Under this scenario, my passport would maintain the illusion that I was in Colombia for another ninety days.

I learned from my earlier mistakes and arrived at the border around 8:30 a.m., when I knew there would be a lot of people I could camouflage myself into. The scariest part, the thing I dreaded most, was either side of that bridge. It was that walk that kept me up at night.

I walked across slowly and when I saw police I looked right at them and smiled. Most of my life I had thought of borders as a physical thing. I thought they were walls and fences and rivers. I was starting to learn otherwise but still held onto the notion that borders were only physical things in specific places. When my feet touched the Colombian side of the border there was still a big part of me that thought the worst was over.

Just Another Gringo in Colombia

I spent the next week in New York celebrating Thanksgiving with family and seeing old friends. My parents always host Thanksgiving and around two dozen guests, from both sides of the family, came to dinner. Every year my dad made a special vegetarian stuffing that I loved and my mom made a green bean casserole with caramelized onions baked on top. Plus, there were boiled parsnips and mashed turnips and lots of other dishes that I only ever had once a year. The table overflowed with homemade dishes others had brought as well. I always put everything together on my plate, topped it with cranberry sauce and mixed it into a multi-colored mush. We all ate until our stomachs felt like bursting.

Thanksgiving has always been my favorite holiday. There are no gifts or consumerism, just family eating together and appreciating what they have. And leftovers.

The next day, after everyone had left I ate another grand meal with just my parents. My dad fried up mashed potatoes and mixed in some corn and stuffing until it was all a golden brown. My mom took out plates and opened a bottle of ketchup. Everyone scooped up a serving onto their plate and we all sat down.

"Are you ready to say prayers?" My mom asked my father.

In unison, my parents made the sign of the cross and began to pray. I sat silently with my hands on my lap. I was raised Catholic but had moved away from religion toward agnosticism after I left for college. My parents were still devout believers though. When they finished we all ate together.

On my last night, rather than waking up early, I never went to sleep, relishing my final hours in the States before hugging my mom goodbye and setting off with my dad for the airport. We arrived early so I had plenty of time to sit and talk with him. "I wish to God you would come home more often," he said.

The previous time I had flown to South America was the first time it was difficult to say goodbye—the first time that the airport symbolized separation rather than just excitement. I began to understand why, per data from the United Nations, only 2% to 3% of the global population lives in a country they were not born in.

My previous flight represented the first time I wasn't just going away on another trip only to someday soon return "home." For the first time, New York had become the trip and Ecuador the home. These words were never spoken, but they sliced through the heavy air that hung between my family and me.

That night I arrived in Bogotá. I was legal in Colombia so there was no reason to worry, yet waiting in line, passport in hand, I surely did not feel relaxed. My passport was quickly filling up with Colombian and Ecuadorian stamps, including one announcing to the world that I had been deported. Furthermore, I was entering Colombia for the purpose of illegally leaving it. Immigration always made me nervous now.

I made it through with no problems, but with only sixty days rather than the ninety I was hoping for. An arbitrary decision made by an unknowing officer that would have great effect on me. I was hoping to put off my next border crossing for as long as possible, so I'd have to apply for an extension before I left the capital.

A *taxista* took me to a hotel tucked away on a side street and walked inside with me. The middle-aged couple stood stiffly behind the desk, though they gave a quick nod to the *taxista*. The man wore a sweater over a collared shirt and parted his hair neatly on the right side; the woman wore a conservative dress and just enough makeup to notice.

"*¿Cuanto cuesta una noche?*—How much does one night cost?" I asked.

They responded in heavily accented English. "Sixty thousand. That means $30 for you."

I was tired and responded in English. "That's too much. It's already late and I will be leaving early. It should be 20,000 or at most 25,000." I took out a wad of pesos from my pocket and reached my hand out. "I can do 30,000."

The couple stood smugly and took the bills. "The cost is 60,000, you can pay me the other half in the morning," the man said.

"That's too much. Give me back the money and I'll look somewhere else," I said. I was exhausted but knew that the couple was ripping me off. Some hotels attempted to double the price for foreigners but usually backed down if you challenged them.

"50,000," he said.

I paid him and went to sleep in my room. When arriving to a foreign city by plane I had come to accept that my first night would be a gross rip-off—nonetheless I slept well on my hard bed and woke up refreshed. The owners of the hotel spoke poor

English and probably assumed I was just another gringo.

Gringo is a term used to describe people from the United States in Latin America, though it is also often used to group together all Westerners. The origin is disputed but the most common story I heard in Ecuador dates it to the Mexican-American war when U.S. soldiers occupying Mexico wore green uniforms. Mexicans would shout "green go!" at the soldiers, which evolved into 'gringo.' Truth is, most people have no idea where it came from and now just use it to group together all the white faces in this foreign land. Latinos that live abroad are sometimes mockingly called 'gringo' when they return to their native country, therefore an accurate modern translation can be 'outsider' or 'foreigner.' Most 'gringos' seemed to embrace the term, or at the very least found it convenient. I never did. A lot of backpackers and expats in South America stuck to a rather narrow trail—often called by those who travel it, The Gringo Trail. They went to the same bars, the same restaurants and the same hidden away mountainside towns where people spoke English and sold Budweiser. I never enjoyed being grouped in with anyone, especially not with people who adhered to the very same culture I was trying hard to leave behind.

When I left to walk around the city, the hotel owners asked me for 10,000 more pesos; I said no and kept walking. I went out hunting for information: cheaper nearby hotels, where to get my visa extended, and transportation to the border. My mission didn't go so well and I ended up just writing an email to my parents and using a pay phone to call Lucía to let everyone know I made it into Colombia without incident. Though by now I had an Ecuadorian cell phone, I never brought it with me on these trips. It didn't fit the character I was playing and would ruin my 'stupid tourist' cover if the police found it during a crossing.

When I returned to my hotel, I decided that I would move to a new room in *el centro* because it was rather residential where I was currently staying.

When I returned to the hotel, the owners were outside in a car and offered to drive me to the visa office, as they were heading that way on an errand. "Of course, you will have to pay us," the man said. I refused. Typically, South Americans are astonishingly friendly and generous people so I hated it when that transformed into greed at the sight of a white face. From the beginning I sensed they saw a dollar sign where I stood rather than a person. When asked again, I swallowed my pride and took them up on their offer, knowing it was my quickest and easiest option.

On the ride we struck up some basic conversation, but it dragged because their English was rather poor and it was clear neither party was genuinely interested in the other.

"What do you do?" the man asked.

"I teach English in Ecuador."

He looked back at me, surprised, and asked, now in his language, "So you speak Spanish?"

"*Sí.*"

"How long have you lived there?" he asked.

"I lived in Cuenca, a city in the south, for a few months, but I have been living in a small city near the capital called Latacunga for over a year now."

"So you work for a program from North America or maybe you are in the Peace Corps?"

"No, I work independently. I came to Ecuador for the first time about two years ago and I liked it so much I just never left. I started teaching English at first because it was the only job available to me, but now I love doing it."

They were clearly impressed with these revelations.

"What is it that you like about Ecuador so much?"

"I like a lot of things. It's so different from where I am from in New York. Where I grew up seems so selfish and self-centered compared to here. Here people have so little, but they share all they have, while there people have so much and give so little." I told them I also liked the stronger sense of community. "Life is simpler here, and for me, I think it's better."

"Do you have a girlfriend in Ecuador?"

With a wide grin on my face, "Yes, I'm on my way back to her right now."

Our excited dialogue continued as the driver bought a round of ice pops for the car from a street vendor in traffic, and we inched closer to our destination. Over the course of the ride their attitudes did a one-eighty, and by the time they dropped me off, they refused my money with a smile before wishing me luck. Though I was certainly happy to shatter their preconceptions, the incident illustrated a larger, less pleasant point.

I had lived my whole life in places where I was in the racial majority. Ecuador was the first place I had been where people so explicitly judged me by how I looked or where I was from. I hated it. The truth is, people treated me better more often than they treated me worse; still, it always made me angry and uncomfortable.

It helped put things into perspective for me. I was upset by the principle of people treating me differently based on some superficial attribute, but charging an extra dollar for lunch is one of the least threatening ways to be discriminated against. In the suburbs of New York City where I grew up, groups of teenagers would sometimes beat up immigrants for fun. While I was living in Latacunga, I heard news reports of a particularly disturbing incident that took place in New York. A young Ecuadorian man, chosen at random and called 'a dirty Mexican' by his teenage attackers, was beaten to death a ten-minute drive from my childhood home.

Losing my Way

A woman working behind the counter at the immigration office in Bogotá gave me a list of things I would need to do before applying for an extension and I spent my day running these small errands. I made photocopies of documents, took new photos and made a small deposit into a government bank account. I returned just before the office closed, but unfortunately one thing that was not mentioned on the list was that I needed to apply with less than 14 days left on the current visa. I was denied.

I decided to get back to Latacunga as quickly as possible which would mean a short domestic flight to Pasto. I called Lucía.

"I'll be home tomorrow," I told her.

In the morning, I wandered out for food, finding *arepas de choclo* (corn patties) and coffee. From previous trips I learned that the best coffee was sold on the street from people carrying it in jugs. In the U.S. and everywhere else I had previously sampled the drink, it was bitter and I wondered why so many people drank it daily. Almost every day when I stopped by Ana's shop, her mother would bring me coffee. It was instant and tasted the same as it ever had, but since I always had to turn down *La Señora's* cooking because it tended to have meat, I made it a point to accept her coffee. She would stand over me and say "Drink it;

drink," in a whiny voice until I took my first sip, then she would laugh manically as she headed back to her own flower shop a few doors down.

The coffee bean grows within a berry and is quite sweet when fresh, and the coffee that comes out of the jugs on the street in Colombia is as fresh as you can get, so it's actually not bitter at all.

While I was sipping my coffee, I came across a closed block filled with police and media centered around a small residential building that had suffered a large explosion. The entire second floor of a four-story building was blown out with pieces of furniture and bricks randomly strewn across the street. Police in the area searched everyone with any sort of bag—which included me and my backpack. FARC and other rebel groups mostly operated in rural areas, but occasionally set off bombs in the capital.

Bogotá had the occasional violence but, along with most Colombian cities, it was somewhat isolated from the conflict. Much of the worst fighting took place in the rural south of the country—often on or near the Ecuadorian border. In 2008 the two nations nearly went to war when Colombian troops briefly invaded Ecuador and killed FARC's second in command, Raúl Reyes, along with twenty others. The group was staying at a FARC camp three kilometers away from the border, inside Ecuador, when the attack occurred.

*

In 2017, as this book went to press and after more than sixty years of violence, FARC is laying down their arms. They have been in decline for years; still, they controlled vast stretches of rural Colombia and counted on thousands of armed fighters, even in their decline. Under the terms of the peace deal FARC will become a political party and will initially be guaranteed a minimum number of seats in the Senate and Congress.

It's possible the two sides can fall toward violence once more, as they did in the failed truce in the 1980s, but there is reason to hope that this time the peace will last. After decades of isolation, in peace Colombia is fast becoming a hot tourist destination and is building out its infrastructure.

Colombia's conflict is complicated though. FARC and the government have always been the two major forces but it has never been just them. A smaller leftist guerilla group, Ejército de Liberación Nacional –National Liberation Army, or ELN, is still at war with the government. The two sides, however, are already in peace negotiations hosted by Ecuador.

*

I took a taxi to the airport and bought a one-way ticket to Pasto.

Once we landed I hopped into another taxi heading toward the border town of Ipiales. There were three other passengers from my flight inside the taxi; two men and one woman. As with most everything in South America, the community pooled its resources in order to more cheaply and efficiently share them, so Colombian taxis were almost always communal. Along the way an accident turned the mighty Pan-American Highway into a beautiful winding parking lot and delayed our journey a few hours.

In Ipiales, I changed $15 to pesos to get me through dinner, a hotel, and crossing the border in the morning. Ipiales is a disgusting border town overrun with thieves, cocaine, guns and *niñas* (prostitutes), but it's also very cheap. I was familiar with a good cross-section of hotels and restaurants from previous escapades, so I spent 16,000 pesos ($7) for a nice hotel and got the city's best pizza. In previous trips I had stayed in places for half of what I paid that night, but I wanted to sleep well before my nerve-racking morning. I settled into a comfortable bed and read a book, *Coyotes,* by Ted Conover, that coincidently was about illegally crossing borders.

Conover had similar ideas to the ones I was forming. As an investigative journalist, he worked and lived with Mexican migrants in Arizona. He then followed a few of them back across the border, into Mexico, to visit their families and see the things they left behind. It was a much more nuanced view of borders and refreshing to read.

I had told lots of people back in the U.S. about that first time on the Colombian border, when Lucía and I sat in an office that hung above *Río Carchi* and bribed the police officer. And that's how most people understood it—just two sides of a river.

Lying to the Police

The next morning around 9:00 a.m., I got into a cooperative taxi headed toward the border. I consulted with the driver to ensure that the taxi would cross the bridge into Ecuador. Crossing the bridge on foot would mean a higher likelihood of police questions, and I was afraid that the next time I lied to the police I would be caught. As expected, the taxi was stopped at the far end of the bridge when it crossed into Ecuador. While the trunk was searched I took my passport out of my pocket and held in tightly between my hands, ready to quickly hand it over if asked. Often the police ignored the passengers and only checked cargo and I hoped that I wouldn't have to speak to the police officer at all. If he did demand my passport, a lack of suspicion would probably mean he would just flip through the pages without looking too closely. After glancing in the trunk the police officer scanned the inside of the taxi. I saw his eyes move from my face down to the passport in my hands. Then he waved us ahead, never asking for our documents.

The taxi dropped us off at the parking lot across from immigration and I quickly climbed into a communal van with a dozen and a half others and exited at the bus station in Tulcán. I felt safe now, and a wave of relief washed over me. Crossing the border involved hours, even days of stressful anticipation, but it was almost all waiting; the moments of danger were just flashes, gone almost as soon as they began.

In my head I had tried to anticipate different scenarios that could play out during each leg of the journey. While I wanted to have my passport ready while crossing, I wanted it hidden at all other times, so before boarding the bus bound for Quito, I stuffed it into the pocket of a pair of jeans within my duffel bag. Highway checkpoints usually consisted of a police officer coming onto the bus and asking for everyone's papers, which for me was my passport. Typically, they looked quickly then left, and even when people didn't have any identification it rarely seemed to be an issue.

Unfortunately for me, the rapidly changing political climate and the rise of nationalism had begun to permeate the police and immigration forces, which were becoming more hostile to foreigners with each passing day. My visa issue was confusing, but the revolution was almost certainly the indirect reason behind my deportation. It bred a fierce brand of nationalism that targeted the nation I came from, and I felt it everywhere I went.

From immigration officials and police officers, down to kids on the street begging for change, everyone had begun to look at me differently.

Though I was oblivious to it at the time, when I viewed myself as a victim, it's worth noting that while I believe all nationalism is bad it's not all equal. It's not that simple. The U.S. has a long history of asserting itself and its values in Latin America, from supporting the brutal coup and dictatorship of Augusto Pinochet in Chile to the possible assassination of Jaime Roldós in Ecuador. In Ecuador nationalism is often a knee jerk reaction contained within its borders, which is bad but Nazi Germany and their plans for the Aryan race were also driven by nationalism. It doesn't justify an Ecuadorian treating me with ire, but it also doesn't mean that all nationalism is equal. Still, it was on the rise in Ecuador and I was beginning to feel it everywhere I went.

The relief and relative safety I felt after bypassing immigration at the border was an outdated illusion. Though I was slow to realize it, always reluctant to believe that the revolution had its dark side, traveling within Ecuador was becoming dangerous for me as well.

I boarded a bus for the five-hour journey to Quito and asked to put my bag in the storage underneath. Instead, I was instructed to board the bus with my bag and to put it near the front in an open space. I took a seat a couple of rows behind. At six feet tall, my height was ordinary where I came from, but I was a giant in Ecuador and the buses were not made for me. As a result, I had to slouch down to avoid hitting my head on the low ceiling when I walked down the aisle, and invent creative poses to fit my legs into the space the seat provided.

Long distance buses, such as this one, kept to a strict

schedule and would start moving at the appointed time, even if empty. Most people never purchased tickets, opting instead to wave down the lumbering machine along the route. Some bus stations charged a ten-cent tax and at these stations you were likely to find a large cluster of passengers waiting just outside the gates. The buses weren't built for luxury, though this one was in fairly good shape. When I sat down I couldn't help noticing how similar the cushioned seats were to those on the discount airline I flew down on, though the plane was much cleaner. The seat covers on the bus were beginning to fray and were caked with spilt food and dirt from the hundreds of passengers who came before me. A handful of passengers boarded the bus as we left town, but two-thirds of the seats remained empty when we pulled onto the highway.

At the first checkpoint two officers boarded the bus. The first man was middle-aged and his uniform was crisp as if it had just been ironed. A younger policeman followed closely behind. The officer with the crisp uniform stopped at each person and asked, "Papers?" while holding out his hand, reviewed the document and moved on in just a few seconds. The policeman behind him followed but didn't speak. The first officer changed his routine when they approached me.

"*¿Hablas español?*" he asked.

I acted confused. "What?"

"Do you speak Spanish?"

"Oh, ummm a little," I replied with the worst Spanish accent and grammar that he could understand.

The older officer gave a wry smile and turned to his partner and resumed speaking in Spanish. "You get this sometimes. These gringos come here and don't know any Spanish—they expect us to speak English even though we're in Ecuador."

The younger officer nodded.

"Passport."

I handed him a photocopy of its first page.

"And where is the original?"

"It good, my passport, yes." I said with a smile, purposefully stumbling on my Spanish and stupidly pointing to the paper in his hand.

"Where are you coming from?"

"Tulcán to Quito," I said, straining to mispronounce the names.

Again, he turned to his partner. "Technically we can't accept this," he said, holding up the photocopy. "But you'll see this all the time; stupid tourists who don't speak Spanish, or have their passport or anything else. They should learn the rules here, but it's not really a problem. I'm sure this gringo is just on vacation." He then handed me back the paper and continued to the next person. It was all just as I expected.

Before leaving the bus, the pair of police asked whose bag was at the front.

I was silent, still playing the role of someone who doesn't speak the language.

The older officer looked at me and asked again, pointing to the bag then to me to illustrate his point.

"Me," I said, nodding my head.

He smiled, but it was anything but friendly. He motioned me forward with his fingers.

While I stood over him, he unzipped the bag and began taking out the clothes and putting them on the dirty floor. While he was laying a pair of jeans down, he felt the passport through the pocket and took it out, holding it up in one hand and looking at me. His smile had faded, and his eyebrows narrowed. His eyes glared.

Fuck, this is horrible, I thought, while trying to maintain my composure. I felt my lungs fill with oxygen and a rush of blood pulse through my body. My mind went into overdrive and in a split second a million thoughts raced through my head as I struggled to keep up the appearance of someone who had no idea what they were doing. With each possible scenario I constructed, I analyzed the potential outcome.

He not only had the grenade that was my passport in his hand, he had reason to be suspicious, and it was clear I was not on my way to immigration.

This could be bad, I thought. It could be jail, it could be deportation, it could be the end of Lucía, the end of Ecuador. He may arrest me; I may spend years in a South American jail.

A sentence of deportation away from the border or airport was the nightmare scenario. At best it would be a longer detention during processing. At worst, a second and blatant violation so soon after my first would have led to full prosecution and a criminal conviction of between three and five years in an Ecuadorian prison. How would my parents find out? How would Lucía find out? Fuck, this is bad.

The first flash was a nightmare, but in the next instant my mind raced into more hopeful territory. As the officer gripped my passport and glared at me, opening his mouth to speak, I felt prepared. He may turn me around and send me to Colombia. If he sends me to the border I will be ecstatic. I will call Lucía and tell her I am delayed and try my luck again at night with a new shift. If he wants to arrest me I will try to bribe him.

Before the first sounds of his response hit my ear, I decided that if he realized the full extent of what I was doing then I would show my hand and try to buy my way out but until that point, I would keep playing the role of the stupid tourist.

He leaned over me and asked with definite anger in his voice, "Why didn't you want to show this to me?"

I gave him a look that said I had no idea what he was talking about and once again pointed at the copy in my hand and said, "My passport, it's good, yes."

He opened up my passport and flipped through the pages starting from the back. A few pages in he saw the entry visa into Colombia and noticed that there was no stamp from Ecuador, but he didn't flip back far enough to see my deportation stamp.

"You are coming from Colombia," he shouted, half as a statement and half as a question.

For the first time I acted as if I understood something and quickly responded "Colombia, yes."

"Why didn't you tell me you were traveling from Colombia when I asked you before?"

The character I was playing wouldn't have understood Spanish, so I gave him a confused look, like a dog that doesn't know where the ball went, half cocking my head.

"Why didn't you tell me you were coming from Colombia? Why!" he shouted.

I meekly responded, "I don't know," but strained to give the impression that I just didn't understand.

He seemed frustrated and focused his attention on my bag. He searched everything, finding some relics from Colombia in the process. After the search, he gave me back my passport and slowly told me that when I enter Ecuador I need a stamp or otherwise I would be fined when I left. He knew that I was missing my entry stamp, but didn't realize that I was sneaking in.

I asked, "I need return?"

With tired disdain in his voice he said, "No, you're an

American so you can just get it in Quito." Still thinking I couldn't understand more than a smattering of Spanish words, he shook his head and muttered to his partner, "I hate these fucking gringos," as they stepped off the bus.

An uncontrollable joy broke out within me and I laughed out loud. I wondered if the other passengers, who had all been watching and listening to the interaction, had suspicion of my reality. Eager to prevent a repeat of what just happened I went through my bag and removed everything that could link me to Colombia: business cards, ticket stubs, customs forms, and so on. Then I threw them out the window.

One thing I hated about Ecuador and Colombia was how freely people littered. I made it a point not to absorb this aspect of their culture, but for that moment I made an exception. Since my deportation I had begun to make a number of 'exceptions.'

Besides the roadside litter I created, there were several items that I didn't want the police to see but still needed to hold on to: my passport, a few thousand pesos, and the visa extension papers. On the seat in front of me, I removed the plastic panel where the seat back and bottom met, put these items inside, and replaced the panel in its original place.

Over the next two hours we encountered three more police checkpoints. I became extremely stressed at each, hoping the other passengers would not betray me if I had to tell a different story to a new officer. My heart pounded as though I'd just sprinted a marathon, and I wished I had switched buses. Luckily, police only boarded the bus once more and didn't give me any trouble. The two other stops had different focuses: one was to check the driver and the other verified the cargo underneath.

The bus pulled into the city of Ibarra shortly after the fourth checkpoint and I knew I'd be safe from there on out. The road between Ibarra and Colombia was hemmed in by mountains and had no detours, so all checkpoints were on this stretch. Ibarra had a few smaller roads to domestic destinations and the police almost never checked buses south of the city.

I stretched my legs in the station while the bus waited for more passengers. When the bus started again I remembered the things I had hidden in the seat back. I had changed seats and now had to climb over a portly indigenous woman to recover my stash. Back at the new seat, the man sitting across the aisle from me had been watching and when I returned he asked if he might see my passport, which was still in my hand. I knew he was probably just curious, but I'd developed a constant paranoia on these trips and thought he might be a cop. I quickly reasoned that if he was, I couldn't deny I had the document, and he could force me to hand it over, so I complied. I watched him carefully as he flipped through the pages, and then handed it back to me with a "Thank you."

When we arrived in Quito I immediately hopped on a new bus heading south. I had recently begun telling the bus drivers I was a student in order to cheat them for a discounted rate— another 'exception' I had begun to make.

The deportation had wiped out any meager savings I had and caused me to lose my job, and money had been an issue ever since. At the time, I told myself the deportation directly caused my financial troubles so I justified a cheaper fare as part of the larger effort to hold onto my once charmed life there. But the bus drivers had nothing to do with my trouble. Most buses were privately owned and operated like small family businesses—so when I cheated bus fares, it probably meant I was just cheating the overworked driver struggling to pay back the loan he took out to buy the bus. It's hard to pinpoint exactly when the fantasy began, but at some point I began to ignore what was right in front of me if it didn't conform into the larger narrative that all was grand and that I was just.

It was the same with Lucía. I knew she had been dishonest, but I thought it was someone else's fault. If she had told me the truth the first night we would not have gotten together. The water was boiling already, but I had been in the pot too long to realize I would burn.

I arrived in Latacunga as the sun faded into the earth and day gave way to night.

While walking home, my heart pounded harder than at any other time that day—no longer in fear of being separated from *mi amor*, but now in anticipation of being with her. At our apartment I walked in the open door. Lucía ran to me and our lips met. I was alone with everything in my arms—and nothing else mattered.

Crossing Three

January 25, 2007

The Agony of Borders

I spent Christmas and New Year's at the edge of the Amazon with Lucía and her family. I loved meeting and becoming comfortable with everyone, and was also fascinated by the new traditions I experienced. The year before I had spent my first New Year's Eve in Ecuador and wandered the streets with Ana's family. On each corner there were life-sized dolls filled with sawdust, and at midnight they fueled a bonfire at every intersection. People took old clothes from a close friend or family member to dress the mannequin and hung it outside someplace public for everyone to see. Each doll represented the person whose clothes they were dressed in. It was playful and mocking, but also somewhat of an honor. At the start of the new year, when your doll burned, it symbolized a new beginning, the cleansing of your sins. Some people wrote lists of their regrets from that year and threw them into the flames. The first days of the new year were filled with practical jokes, something like April Fool's Day in the U.S., and whenever you were caught, the traditional response was, "I'm innocent," and everyone laughed. Starting fresh, starting innocent each year, was a concept that really appealed to me.

As fun as the New Year's festivities were, the big event that week was Christmas Eve or *Nochebuena* (the good night). It felt more like Thanksgiving to me: there was a big meal and lots of family, but there was no tree, no holiday sales at the mall, no stockings to fill, and no pile of gifts to wrap. All we gave to Lucía's parents was a framed picture of us together. We'd visited a friend of mine in the Amazon for my birthday and he snapped the shot when we weren't looking. We were laughing, my mouth open and hers in a wide grin, gazing into each other's eyes, while a monkey wrapped his tail around my neck and his arms around Lucía's waist, pulling us together.

We ate the big meal in Lucía's parents dining room. The small room was empty save the table and the yellow walls had no decoration or ornaments except for a massive, wood-framed bronze relief of the last supper. There was a Christmas tablecloth and four red candles burning on top. While the table was almost too large for the room, it was not large enough for the family. Lucía's child sat on her lap and her nieces piled on their mother. We settled in for dinner at midnight and began by standing for a round of toasts. Lucía's mother, Mayra, went first:

"I look around the table and I am so grateful to have everyone here, so happy that all of us can come together today— but we are not whole. There will always be a place at this table for Maria and Paul and I wish that one day I can have all of my family here with me. I wish that we could all be together again."

Lucía had been telling me about her family for weeks. The five children and two parents were all very close, if not always together. Her father spent much of her childhood living and working illegally in the United States in order to send money home, and since his return, two of the family's children had left.

Lucía's sister had taken a vacation to the U.S. a few years earlier, met a man, and married. She wed her husband without changing her status and asking permission from immigration and when her visa ran out, she was considered illegal. If she ever left the U.S., she wouldn't be able to return. Before I had heard her story, I—like many Americans—had believed that marriage was a legal loophole to immigration, that when two people wed they automatically gained citizenship to each other's countries. The reality, at least in the case of Ecuador, was starkly different.

After my deportation Lucía and I spoke more seriously about marriage visas and I had done a good bit of research into it. In the case of me and Lucía, it would have likely taken over two years to run through the multi-step process. It would also cost a few thousand dollars. A good lawyer could grease all the wheels and do much of the legwork but that would be even more money. Deep pockets always made immigration less of a hassle.

I also learned that most nations offer their own version of the 'investment visa.' In Ecuador you needed to deposit $25,000 in an Ecuadorian bank; in the U.S. it's an investment of $500,000 or more in a U.S. based business (called the EB-5 'Alien Investor' visa, which also puts you on the fast track to full citizenship). Most people pay *coyotes* or bribe police, but the rich just need to make a deposit into their own bank account.

My own experiences and research taught me that while it is often easy to independently visit other nations, it is usually problematic to live there independently. If you work for a government, corporation or NGO and have their support, or if you have a lot of money, everything is streamlined, but borders are less kind to individuals.

In Ecuador, for however long the marriage visa process took—and I found one couple who told me theirs lasted seven years—I would not be allowed to leave the country. So it was inconvenient and expensive but there was a much bigger issue that kept us waiting—Lucía was still married. Every time I asked her about it she told me there were just small details to take care of and everything would be finalized "in a few weeks." It made my visa options unclear and put both that and our relationship into a holding pattern.

In addition to a sister in the United States, Lucía's brother was similarly stranded in Europe by work and love. In a culture that placed such a high value on family, borders so often tore them apart. Mayra's speech struck a chord with the table and a somber air hung over the group as I began my short monologue. I told everyone how touched I was that they welcomed me into the family with such open arms, and water began to fill my eyes, forcing me to stop abruptly. I'm not sure if my tears were from pleasure or pain. I was overjoyed to be a part of such a special and intimate moment with my new family, yet there was a certain emptiness because of the distance I felt from my family in New York.

*

After missing a full semester of work at UTC because of my deportation, I was rehired and began working again after the new year. I was able to earn some much needed money by teaching an intensive seminar during the semester break and would work regularly again in the new semester starting in February.

Almost a year earlier, when I had first seen my students on the streets, choking on tear gas but holding their ground fighting for a better tomorrow, I had been proud. The students' noble struggle became the national cause and the tiny party with influence at the university exploded, and everyone rushed to it.

Now I had a new boss—one whose background was more political than educational. Qualified teachers were being replaced by men and women whose only qualification seemed to be their ability to hang up large amounts of propaganda each night. The university I once held in such high esteem seemed more and more like a political tool rather than a leader in the fight for free public education.

President Correa had taken office and his army in the streets grew larger by the day. Congress tried to block his power grabs, and in response, the nation watched dramatic live television coverage as his supporters surrounded Congress and fought their way in. When politicians tried to meet in other cities, Correa's new citizens' army would instantly appear and chase them away. *El Universo* was full of headlines on the power struggle: *Protesters Continue to Block the District Attorney's Office; Correa Supporters Take to the Street to Support a New Constitution; Demonstrators Interrupt Session of the National Election Committee.*

"Correa was the first politician I believed in," Ana said to me as we discussed the latest flash mob that violently attacked the opposition. "But he's just like the rest. He's turning into a dictator."

"Yeah, he's definitely not what I had hoped he would be, but maybe he will still come around," I replied.

Ana lifted her head from the flowers she was pruning and rolled her eyes. "He's no good, and you know that as well as me. You'll admit that soon enough."

Opposition leaders began fleeing the country, mostly to Colombia, and *la Revolución Ciudadana* steamrolled forward, consuming everything in its path.

In mid-January Lucía met her husband and his lawyer in Ambato to discuss their much-delayed divorce. I was reading in bed when she came home.

"Hola amor." She greeted me cheerfully as she put down her bag and came over to give me a kiss.

"Hola… So, how did it go?"

She sighed. "It was alright. It should all be finished in a few weeks."

"But that's what you said a few weeks ago."

"I know, and I'm sorry. He was being difficult. He also said that he wanted to hire someone to kill you."

"What?! What do you mean?"

"Yeah, he said he was looking for someone."

"What?! He wants to kill me?"

"I told you he was being difficult." She shrugged.

"Well, this is different. Is this serious?"

"I don't know. He is military but maybe he just said that to make me upset."

"You don't seem very upset about it."

*

Lucía woke me up from a nightmare at 6:40 a.m. We were already behind schedule. It was the 25th of January and my Colombian visa was set to expire the following day. I wanted to be at the border by lunch; and Lucía was late for work. I started getting ready as quickly as I could. Our shower was broken, so I used the one downstairs. Normally I would just skip it, but before setting off on a trip of this nature, where anything seems possible, it's good to be clean. Our landlord yelled at me for using his shower, then I returned to our apartment and Lucía yelled at me because she was going to be late for work. The day was off to a rough start.

Lucía and I had done our best to recover from the terrible fight we had before my deportation, but it was a bumpy road. A couple of weeks earlier we had been out drinking and got into another fight. This time it was because a woman asked me to dance twice—I declined both times but that was enough of a spark. Lucía stormed off, taking my keys, and I followed a minute behind. She locked the door, lay down on the floor of our living room and cut her wrists, all of which I could see through the window. I tiptoed on a ledge that ran alongside the house and climbed into our open bedroom window. We quickly made up, but the next day I broke a little bit. The veneer of my fantasy began to crack.

I wasn't the first person she had dated after her marriage; she had also had an affair with a man from Argentina. That relationship never got very serious but she told me she thought about suicide when that ended.

"You need to call your mom," I told her. "You need to tell her everything."

"No."

"Baby, I love you, but I can't do this anymore."

"What are you talking about?"

"You really scared me last night. I don't want anything bad to happen to you."

"I was fine."

"You need to have someone to talk to when you're angry with me. I need help, baby. I need this. Please. For me?"

Looking back, that was probably the beginning of the end. It was the first time I ever had even an inkling of a thought that I wasn't helping Lucía. It was the first time I wanted someone else to step in.

As Lucía and I headed to the bus station, walking silently and standing apart, I was thinking about hitmen hunting me down and Lucía bleeding from her wrists. I was not okay. Somewhere along the way I began to lose my patience and ability to always see the bright side of things. Part of me wanted to blame Lucía because it's easier to not take responsibility, but honestly I was more prone to fighting and less likely to forgive than I had been just a few months before. I was trying to cope with a lot; and so was she.

190

We boarded a bus for Lasso, the small industrial town on the way to Quito where Lucía had recently started an unpaid internship.

"I'm sorry baby, I just hate these trips," I told her.

"I know. And I'm still upset with Veronica. I'm sorry too," she said.

That week Lucía had interviewed for a high-paying job and was told that the position was hers pending approval from the company board. After hearing her good news, Veronica used a family contact to land the job for herself instead.

"She is a dog," I said. And we both laughed. Calling her a *perra*, a dog, was a strong insult and had become my unofficial nickname for Veronica since she and Lucía had their falling out.

Just as I had deflected all the blame away from Lucía and toward her husband, we had collectively begun to blame Veronica for further troubles. Sure, some of that ire was deserved, but in hindsight it seems clear that we were also avoiding taking responsibility for ourselves. All would eventually all catch up to us.

While the bus sped away from Latacunga, Lucía leaned against me and buried her head into my shoulder. I moved my hand across her body and over her shoulder and squeezed into a hug, then left my arm draped over her. We kissed as she got off at the rose plantation where she was interning; and I was alone.

I got off a few minutes later and transferred to a new bus headed to Quito. Every few minutes the bus would slow down just enough to allow someone to jump on or off, occasionally coming to a full stop for larger groups or for farmers transporting sacks of food to some distant marketplace. The sacks were quickly thrown into the bus, or more often, thrown on top of it. A young man carrying a chicken upside down by its tied feet sat down next to me, and the bus began to fill. As we approached the modern capital, the stops became more frequent, and university students, backpacks slung over their shoulders, stood in the aisle as the empty seats disappeared. Once into the sprawl that stretched endlessly south from the city's center, new vendors jumped on each time the bus slowed. Over the drone of the diesel engine and conversation they squeezed themselves through the crowded aisle and back again, calling out whatever product they happened to be selling. When I heard the familiar cry of *"¡Papas!¡Papas!"* I bought my meager breakfast in exchange for fifty cents.

By now this scene was familiar, but when I first arrived in South America, both the chaos and extreme utility of the region's buses had amazed me. Shortly after I finished my oversized bag of homemade potato chips the bus pulled into the capital's main bus station. Amid hundreds of these old machines that kept the country moving, I tried to plan my return from the border and asked around when buses would stop running to Latacunga that night. Whenever asking for a bus schedule, directions or anything of that nature, everyone had their own answer, so it was best to get a few opinions and take the average. With this method I had a vague idea that buses would stop at eleven or twelve and start again around four or five. Satisfied, I gave a small girl ten cents in exchange for a wad of cheap toilet paper and use of the dirty public bathroom she sat in front of. Unless it was an emergency, I avoided doing anything that would necessitate the use of that complimentary, but always insufficient, wad of paper. Plumbing was not one of the nation's strong points and flushing usually meant dipping a bucket into some giant container of dirty water. Even with the soiled paper thrown into its own bucket in the stall, the toilets were still prone to clogging. Sometimes there were urinals, and other times just a trough, but either way, taking a piss seemed far more sanitary.

With my bladder emptied I was ready for a long and uncertain bus journey. I walked back onto the road where I knew I could hop onto a bus heading north. About halfway there, in the city of Ibarra, for a reason that was never explained, we were all made to switch buses. That is where my real journey began. The other side of Ibarra was where the police checkpoints were located and the dangers of my situation were exposed.

All week I had traded sleep for anxiety, lying in bed thinking of stories I could tell and roles I could play if questioned by police. This was undoubtedly the cause of the nightmares that haunted me when I was able to drift into an awkward unconsciousness. Each day I devised new plans and held them against the older ones. On the bus, I put them all together and debated, in long drawn-out internal dialogue, which story I would use.

Most versions of the character I played were not able to speak Spanish, and I had to keep that consistent. The bus rides were solitary adventures where I had nowhere to turn but inside, so I pored over my recent life and the dangers I was in. I lost my mind but kept a dumb smile on my face.

We all wear masks, but if you wear the same one for too long for too many people, it can begin to consume the face behind it. Somewhere in the last few months I had forgotten who I was.

It was difficult to dig myself out of the financial hole I found myself in after my deportation—more difficult than I thought it would have been. Besides the occasional work in Ana's shop, *la Señora* took me on long bus rides toward the Amazon where we would pick orchids and other flowers to sell in Latacunga.

The 'tutoring' work Kleaber helped me find quickly mutated

into something far less noble: I began just doing students homework, which paid better. Not long before, I would have considered this work immoral, but after a while I barely hesitated when new clients came my way. In a short time, I went from someone who helped others learn to someone who helped them cheat. I also made deals with local travel agencies to steer clients their way and started selling marijuana to these same tourists. I gradually reduced my volunteering at INNFA until I stopped going altogether to have more time to make money in whatever way I could. But it wasn't just about freeing time. In the beginning at INNFA I tried my best to be understanding and kind, someone the children might learn from, and I didn't want them to see what I was turning into.

I stopped doing what I believed in and replaced that void with things that made me feel guilty and wicked. I did whatever I could to keep the dream alive. I was paranoid, scared and desperate, and somehow, amidst that, I reasoned that the best way to get back to the values that had made my life so fulfilling was to completely abandon them.

I hated it. I hated all of it, but I told myself it was necessary and only temporary.

*

I was very tense. This trip seemed less risky than previous ones, but I'd come to learn that what happens at immigration will only be certain when written in past tense. The various branches of immigration in each nation were only consistent in the sense that they consistently gave me different and often contrary instructions; and the crossing at Rumichaca had never been nice to me.

We passed San Gabriel, the last town before Tulcán. The countryside between these two outposts was the most likely place for a checkpoint. I'd been on this stretch of road before, but I remembered it being shorter. I stared out the window into the rain and it seemed we would never arrive. When it rained in this part of the Andes, it was cold and miserable, and no one, not even the police, wanted to stand outside in that unless it was absolutely necessary. I was never so happy to see rain at ten thousand feet.

I readied my story and prepared for interrogation. I decided on a version that, in some ways, mirrored the truth. I would speak Spanish. First show the photocopy and hope it would end there. This was the first part of every plan. If asked for my passport, which was likely, I would calmly hand it over and hope for an unknowing officer who would mindlessly flip through the pages without a second glance.

Everyone assumes that Americans don't get deported, and I was able to use that to my advantage. There was some sneaking and always the potential for confrontation, but more than anything else, it was a mental exercise. However, there was a very real physical danger involved, and perhaps an even larger perceived one, which was constantly on my mind. Every time I crossed, I risked jail and a forced separation from the dream life that was already slipping out of my control.

At first I only worried about getting caught when I was crossing, but eventually these thoughts and the possible consequences permeated my subconscious and stayed with me every single day. The whole process was incredibly nerve-racking and frightening, but through it all, as I nearly pissed in my pants, I had to keep my head up, walk confidently and smile.

I had my lies carefully prepared . . .

If the officer realized I was illegal, I would claim to have been in Colombia since my deportation, only entering Ecuador a few days ago. I would say that the *taxista* at the border told me I could skip the long lines at immigration by getting my stamp in Quito. I took his advice and went straight to the capital. While there, I met a friend from high school who does administrative work for the Peace Corps. My friend has a lot of connections with the U.S. Embassy (implying that now I did too, which I hoped would make them hesitate to arrest or deport me) and arranged a meeting with a friend of his. At the embassy I learned I could in fact get my stamp in Quito, but I first needed my exit stamp from Colombia, which I was just now returning to do.

If prompted, I had worked out all the details for my fictitious life, and I was more than ready to play that role. I thought this plan was pretty solid with a minimal chance of failure, but just as every plan begins with silently handing over a photocopy, every plan ends with a bribe.

Thanks largely to the rain and a bit of luck, we made it to Tulcán without ever being stopped. I asked about the bus schedule and got a taxi to the border. I walked across the bridge into Colombia. The rain had subsided and I stood on the bridge, looking down into the deep gorge and the water flowing through it that divided these nations. I let the rush of water drown out all other noise. This place seemed safe. There were no police actually on the bridge, only at its edges. When, for a week in August, both countries refused to accept me and I made dozens of crossings back and forth, this bridge represented an island of tranquility—it was the only place I felt safe, the only place I could exist.

Raising my head and reluctantly moving each foot forward, I let the noise of the world flash back in and entered Colombia. I got my exit stamp and within five minutes I was back on the bridge. Seemingly, my journey was now halfway over. So far everything was going perfectly, but I knew the greatest challenge was still ahead.

My deportation order was for only the calendar year[4], so theoretically the new year marked a fresh start. Traveling through and then exiting Ecuador was the only part I thought was illegal, but I was still frightened. Months earlier, I'd also had that same impression, that my crossing was legal, just moments before I was arrested and deported. In the months since that setback, reality and paranoia had fused together in my mind. While my deportation order had run out, irrational or not, I was scared. Scared that things might get worse; scared that I couldn't cope with further setbacks; scared that the whole house of cards would come tumbling down without a moment's notice. If things didn't go right at immigration in Ecuador, all my stories and plans would end and I would have to retreat to one of the border towns to contemplate my next step, illegal on either side of the bridge.

I waited anxiously on the long line at Ecuador immigration. If my story was asked, I would use the winner from the bus contest, but it would be more cut and dried here, more of a computer's choice than a human's. I thought the machine would be on my side, but I'd been wrong about that before. At the time of my deportation I was told I was banned from entering the country for the calendar year of 2006. Now, three weeks into 2007, one could assume I'd have no trouble getting in, but I had

---

[4] Deportation orders usually have end dates: one year, five years, ten years and life are the most common. Like a jail sentence, the amount of time varies by nation and violation.

learned to never assume anything at immigration, especially during a nationalist upsurge.

The line for immigration spilled out of the building and into the open mountain air. I took out my notebook and wrote until the rain returned and smeared my ink. Once inside I resumed writing until a friendly Colombian behind me started a conversation. I was grateful for the distraction.

"*¿Eres estadounidense?*—Are you an American?" he asked.

"*Sí.*"

"I've always wanted to go to your country."

"It's good to travel and see new places, but I love it here," I said.

"Well it's not as easy for Colombians to travel. You're lucky, you can just live in my country or Ecuador and you won't have any problems."

I forced a smile. It was my turn in line, "Good luck," I said, and walked to the counter.

The heavyset officer, whose threat of jail had been ringing in my ears for the past year, was nowhere to be seen. Across the counter stood a thinner man who looked tired and bored. I handed over my passport.

He meticulously reviewed it. The tension mounted. He stared at my deportation stamp, and then went through every page, running his fingers over the dozen visas Ecuador had already granted me. He seemed uncertain what to do. My heartbeat raced and my palms sweat, but my face kept a smile. He entered more information into his computer, squinted at the screen, and then, without ever saying a word, gave me my new stamp. At first I hid my joy, but then I realized: I didn't have to hide anything or wear any mask, at least not at that moment. A huge smile grew across my face as I walked away from the counter.

I quickly got a taxi to the bus station and jumped on a bus as it pulled away from the frontier. On the bus I met a nice Colombian woman living in Ecuador. She was in her late thirties, and had the body of an aerobics instructor, each curve on her body blending into the next. She had a taut face with wide lips, wore tight black pants showing off her well-defined calves, and had flowing, curly black hair that looked fresh from the shower even though it was bone dry. I sat down in the seat across from her and let out a sigh of relief.

"*¿Cómo supo usted que podría saltar en el autobús así?*—How did you know you could just jump on the bus like that? I've never seen a white person do that here. Do you live in Tulcán?" She leaned over inquisitively.

"Well, I've been here a lot." I said, grinning at her. I was feeling confident, so after a short pause I added, "I was fixing my visa at the border."

"Yeah, I lived in the United States for a few years and had a lot of trouble with immigration there so I know how it must be for you in Ecuador with this new government." Then she looked at me, the same way that I had looked at her before I told her I had to fix my visa. "I was deported," she said.

I laughed. "Me too. That's really why I was at the border, but today for the first time since the deportation, I am legal in Ecuador. What happened to you?"

"I met an American who was doing business in Colombia and we traveled to his country together. We got married there, but we never filed any papers with the embassy and my visa expired so I was illegal. I kept asking him to help me fix my status, but he never did. I don't think he wanted to. He started to hit me, but I couldn't call the police because I didn't want to get deported. So I stopped having sex with him and stayed with friends on the weekends when he was home the most." Her eyes narrowed and she grit her teeth. "He found a new Colombian to fuck and called the police on me. When they checked my status they tried to deport me, but I fought them."

"What happened?" I asked.

"I hired the only lawyer I could afford and got them to review my case. I was married to an American and I had a right to stay. They kept me in a jail cell the whole time. We lost the case but I appealed even though I knew I would lose again. I spent eighteen months in jail until they flew me back to Colombia."

"I'm sorry. But why did you continue to fight if you knew you would lose?" I asked.

"I had done nothing wrong. What was my crime?" She paused before she went on, now looking down, "It just wasn't right."

She was a brave woman. We exchanged numbers to keep in touch and wished each other luck.

I rode buses all night and arrived back in Latacunga at 2:00 a.m., nineteen hours after I had left it. It was raining as I walked the deserted downtown streets of the small colonial city to my house. The fairytale life I was living just a few months before was long gone, and yet, soaking wet and walking in the middle of the street the whole way, I felt euphoric. I attributed so many of my problems to my border troubles, and desperately wanted to believe that now things could go back to how they were before.

At our house Lucía was studying and still awake. She jumped up and wrapped her arms around me when I walked in and I thought maybe it would be alright.

Crossing Four

March 29, 2007

Giving Up on Hope

I could argue that I got deported at a bad time, but there's no good time to be forced to leave your home. Everyone who is deported is already dealing with a myriad of other issues, just like any other person. Whatever problems I had before became magnified, and much of what made me happy drifted deeper into the cracks.

A few weeks after I got back from my January crossing, there was one particularly disturbing incident. I had just returned to the downtown apartment Lucía and I were renting when I heard the doorbell and the loud screech of tires. By the time I reached the door there was no one outside and no cars in sight, but there was a shoebox on the step. It was crushed, with a tire mark across it. A bright red liquid oozed out of the torn cardboard sides. Curious, I opened the box: inside was a dead and badly disfigured guinea pig. It looked like they had run over the box while the animal was trapped inside, still alive. Blood had splattered on the sides of the cardboard and the animal's intestines poked through the torn skin and fur. The front lip was peeled back and ripped from its face, revealing a handful of broken teeth and slashed gums.

I wanted to vomit and cry at the same time. I felt horrible, and a dozen paranoid thoughts raced through my mind. *Is this because I'm American? Is it someone I know? Do they know that guinea pigs are pets in my country? Did they know I was home? Are they watching me? Did the same people leave the dog shit on the step yesterday? Will they come back?*

The anti-American sentiments I had dealt with before had

been annoying though bearable—but the mutilated guinea pig was the breaking point. After I went back inside and collected myself, I fell into a state of depression and waited for Lucía to come home. But when I told her what had happened, she didn't seem to care. She didn't understand why I was so upset.

"I live here, that's why. This is my home," I shouted at her. "People spit on me in the park and leave dead animals at our door and you don't even care." And for the first time I started to seriously think that maybe this *wasn't* my home, that maybe Lucía wasn't the woman for me, that maybe the dream was just fantasy.

That same week, while I still clung to the idea that things would work out with Lucía and me, with Ecuador and me, I walked past a protest in the park. A hundred youths, faces covered with bandanas, were blocking the road while a group of riot police lined up a block away. The police were putting on their gas masks; the protesters were collecting pieces of pavement and rocks for a counterattack. After I passed the protesters and had my back to them, I heard one yell after me.

"*¡Fuera Yankee!*—Yankee go home."

I turned around and looked in the direction the voice came from.

He said it again. It was the tall one with the red bandana. I turned and walked straight for him. A crowd gathered to watch what would happen.

"What did you say?" I asked.

"Yankee go home," he repeated, though with less confidence in his voice.

I laughed but did not smile, did not break eye contact. "You don't like my country because it treats Ecuador unfairly. Because it doesn't know your nation but it makes assumptions about it. Because it thinks all of Latin America is the same, thinks all

Ecuadorians are the same. Because it thinks it knows you, but it's ignorant." I paused. "You're the same. I live here. I work here. And the U.S. government does not represent me anymore than Lucio represented you. You're the same as the U.S; you're part of the problem."

The man with the red bandana responded in a voice so low that I barely heard him above the din of the protest, "I'm sorry. I didn't know."

I turned my back and walked away. At the time I felt proud, but what if the roles were reversed? What if the protest was in the United States and had anti-immigrant undertones? What if one of the protesters shouted at an Ecuadorian walking by or a Muslim woman in a hijab and that person confronted the crowd?

*

The mobs in the streets who had elected a president were now enforcing the law, chasing away any semblance of resistance. The headlines in *El Universo* seemed worse every day: *Protesters Gather Outside Congress; Congress is Full of Tension and Doubts; Government Will Not Permit Representatives to Enter Congress; American Society of Press Worried About the Freedom of the Press; Political Violence in Rocafuerte; Six Injured in Violence at Congress; Shots Fired Outside the Marriott.*

I sat in a bar, drinking beers with Kleaber, and watched the nation I had fallen in love with break down toward violence. Crowds were attacking opposition politicians. The television ran clips of well-groomed men in gray suits lying on the concrete stairs outside Congress, bleeding from their heads. "My country was never like this before. Ecuadorians are peaceful," Kleaber told me, before tilting his head back and emptying his glass. The hopeful idealism of a year before had turned into a greedy hunger for power. The mobs in the streets began to resemble what they had vowed to replace.

And then there was Lucía. She was my everything, *mi todo*. She was what kept me going, the person I could do anything for, but that fantasy began to unravel along with everything else. I had wanted to change her; I had thought I could help her and mold her into everything I thought she could be. But I slowly began to realize, that's just who she was. I wanted to make her into someone who wasn't real and wondered if she had convinced me of the fantasy, or if I was the one who'd fooled her. She entered my life when I thought that not only was anything possible but that it was probable if there was only enough effort, determination and love.

As everything else was turning sour, I began to realize I was wrong about her. I came home from work one day in early March and found cigarette butts and empty bottles of beer stashed in a cabinet. When I confronted Lucía about it, she lied.

"My friend Maria came over," she said.

"I saw Maria today—and she doesn't smoke."

"Fine, it was another friend. I thought you'd be mad, that's why I didn't tell you. His name is Rene. He's just a friend; I promise."

Rene kept coming over when I wasn't home.

Lucía had lied to me throughout our relationship, and for most of it I believed every word she said. I'm not sure if I stopped loving her because I realized she was lying, or I started seeing her lies because I stopped loving her.

I realized it wasn't just other men in her life that she was lying about; she was lying about everything, even the small stuff that didn't matter. She would watch one movie then tell me it was another, or say she saw someone in the park when I knew they were out of town, or so many other insignificant things. I suppose this was happening all along but I never saw any of it; suddenly, I saw all of it.

I may have even seen more lies than were there. I doubted everything she said to me. I started to doubt my own memory. I didn't know what was real anymore, even in my own life. Even now, years later, I'm not sure which parts of my fairytale life were always fantasy.

I didn't trust her anymore. I didn't love her anymore. I didn't want to go to sleep next to her at night. I didn't want to wake up alongside her.

"I think we need some space," I told her. "This is just temporary. Maybe we can still work this out."

"Promise?"

"I don't know."

That afternoon I told *la Señora* I wanted to move. She didn't ask why. "*Espera*," she said and walked out. When she returned, she handed me a key. "Take this room for now."

Her shop and the buildings behind it were owned by a couple who lived in Quito and rarely visited Latacunga. *La Señora* helped them rent the rooms and collect payment.

That night, I went to sleep alone.

A week later Lucía and I went out together. She had had a meeting with her lawyer that afternoon and she told me that the divorce was finally going to go through. "It will just be a few more days," she said.

"It's always just a few more days away."

"This time it really is just a few days away. We are so close." She was beaming.

Not long before her optimism would have been infectious. It wasn't this time. But Lucía still wanted to celebrate so we went out to a *discoteca*.

We drank too much and I didn't want to dance. Lucía found other men to dance with while I sat and watched from the table. Another girl sat next to me. We said hello to each other. Lucía looked over across the dance floor and came back fuming. "Let's just go home," I told her, trying to avoid a public fight. "I'll walk you."

We left, but fought on the way. It was petty and stupid and continued inside her apartment, onto the bed we used to sleep in together.

"I can't do this anymore," I told her.

She looked at me, rolling her eyes up and pushing her bottom lip out. "Are you leaving me?

"Yes."

"Will you stay here, tonight? Just tonight," she asked through tears.

In the morning, we woke up and she rolled over and kissed me. "*¡Buenos días!*" she said, with a broad smile.

I looked at her, confused by her good mood. "Do you remember last night?"

"Not really. We went dancing then came back here and went to sleep, right?"

"We broke up last night."

Her smile faded and tears welled up in her eyes. "I don't remember that."

I called out sick from my class later that morning and stayed in bed with her so we could break up again.

We lay in bed together, both on our sides facing each other but not talking, not touching. She turned her back to me and scooted closer so her body was pressed against mine, her back against my chest. She grabbed my arm and draped it over her.

"I slept with Rene," she said.

"I know."

"I'm sorry."

"I know."

I felt cold and indifferent to it all. Lying awake that night next to the cemetery, on a bed stained with the sex and sickness of whoever rented the room before me, I just needed to get away.

In the rare moments when life wasn't consuming me, chewing at my still living flesh, I was able to take a step back and look into the mirror. And I hated what I saw.

That first time I had snuck back into Ecuador, I had done it for her; she represented all of my motivation. So much had changed since that day.

The sunflower had wilted away and died.

The Help of Strangers

I still wasn't ready to give up though. Not yet.

In late March 2007, everything seemed to be crumbling around me. Lucía and I were over. My romance with the revolution had turned sour. And I didn't feel I had a home. I left the United States because I didn't feel like I belonged. And it didn't feel like I belonged in Ecuador anymore either. That same nationalism I hoped to avoid when I left my birth nation was now surfacing in Ecuador.

Still, I wanted to stay. Ecuador had once captivated me in a way I'd never felt before.

I could only legally stay in Ecuador 180 days in the calendar year, so if I wanted to live there I needed my passport to lie and claim that I was somewhere else for the remaining 185 days. I still had a few weeks left on my ninety-day visa, but frustrated with my life and where it was going, I really needed to get away. An illegal crossing, once a personal nightmare, had turned into an attractive escape from my everyday life.

I woke up early on a cold rainy day and went to the bus station with plans for crossing another border. This time I would head south, into Peru. I would enter Peru legally then sneak back into Ecuador.

While Colombia was closer, I felt I was pushing my luck at that border—and the Peruvian coast can be so much warmer than the Andes. Latacunga had become much too cold for me. With the travel advice of a dozen drivers at three different bus stations, combined with about ten hours on the road, I finally made it to the closest city to the Peruvian border. I had been to Machala before, but only for a few hours. After a full day on buses I arrived that night, quickly got a $3 hotel, the morning's bus schedule, and went to the park to sit down under an artificial light. I restarted my journal for the first time since my deportation, and hoped I could restart my life which had gone sour when the writing stopped.

The next morning, I got up early and caught an international bus to Tumbes, Peru. The bus stopped at immigration long enough for me to run inside and hand over my passport. I got back on the bus only to realize that I lacked my new exit stamp. The next stop was Huaquillas, a city that straddles the border and lies in both nations with immigration offices on opposite ends of the city.

In 1941, while most of the world was focused on the conflict in Europe, Ecuador and Peru fought a war over their border. Peru won a decisive victory and seized almost half of Ecuador's territory, mostly in the Amazon but also a small strip along the coast. Ecuador declared the peace treaty void in 1960 and there were small clashes along the border for the next three decades. Maps drawn in Ecuador included the area lost to Peru—with Huaquillas fully in Ecuador. The border posts at the crossing were built so far apart because each side had claimed the territory as their own. A small clash in 1995 escalated into the Cenepa War and ended with both nations signing a definitive peace agreement in 1998 and formal demarcation of the entire border in 1999.

I asked a few people for advice and decided I should return to Ecuador to ensure there were no problems. Back in Ecuador they confirmed that I was in the computer and didn't know why the stamp didn't show up. They gave me a new one by hand and sent me on my way. On the deserted road outside immigration a motorcycle appeared on the landscape's arid and barren horizon. When he slowed at the speed bump where I had stationed myself, he offered me a ride to the border for a dollar.

I was dropped off at the border, which is a bridge over a small, polluted stream in the middle of a hectic market. There were tables and booths set up in no particular order, selling everything from fruits and vegetables to black-market gasoline. The same as the Colombian border, savvy consumers flocked to this vast bazaar to exploit competing tax laws. Most of the merchants were poor and wore tattered clothes even while selling brand new ones. Others walked around the scattered mess of tables and semi-permanent structures and whispered the sale of less public goods.

"Hey Mister. You want some cocaine? Real cheap."

"No thanks."

"Maybe a girl? All sorts of pretty girls. What kind you like?"

There was also an abundance of men offering currency exchange, and two of them pounced on me before I was even off the motorcycle. They were both short and husky. One wore a green, translucent visor that gave his face a strange hue and while it looked like he hadn't shaved in a week, I wouldn't yet call it a beard. The other, while clean-shaven and sun-lit, literally licked his lips as he waddled over to me.

Money changers at borders are rarely honest and when I had my money and theirs in hand, halfway through the transaction, I discovered they were scamming me. I took their calculator from them and now, holding all the cards, showed them that I had figured out the con by repeating the trick they had attempted. I typed a number into the calculator and saved it. They had done this first step discreetly before they showed me the calculator. Next I typed in the amount I wanted to exchange ($80) and multiplied it by the rate we had agreed upon (3.2 *Soles* for each dollar). I pressed the equals button and displayed to them the correct amount. Then I replicated their swindle by pressing the button that brought up the saved number rather than the equals button. After I showed them, I returned their money—proud of myself for showing up these thieves at their own game.

Travelers are always targets for thieves and cheats but you can avoid most of it by just obeying common sense. Since these guys already tried to scam me once, I should have walked away. But almost everyone at the border is there to cheat you, so I let them change my money for the correct amount before hailing a taxi to Peru immigration.

When I paid the *taxista* he immediately recognized my bills as false. This was confirmed by police and other *taxistas* as we walked around the immigration office. Both the hundred and fifty were counterfeit, while the smaller currency was legit. One hundred fifty *soles* was a little less than $50 at the current exchange, which was significant to me since I was nearly broke. In my pocket I carried almost all the money I had in the world, which was now reduced to about $80. I went back to the border with the *taxista* to hunt down the counterfeiters. My memory failed me, and they'd probably fled anyway, but during our search we managed to pick up some police and other border creatures who all had their own stories and offered, often conflicting, advice for me. A fistfight nearly broke out between the various parties 'helping me,' and I left quickly. I hate borders.

Back in Peru I got my ninety days, then a van to Tumbes followed by a car to the nearest beach—Zorritos. Zorritos is hardly noteworthy, just a small strip along the coastal road. It's also the first beach in Peru, which is why it became my destination. I got a cheap but clean hotel and went for a swim.

I made quick friends with the staff at a bar on the beach and went out with them that night. I sulked with them about Lucía and my border troubles, and they took me out and tried to cheer me up. They were kind and wanted nothing in return. It was just the sort of thing that made me fall in love with South America in the first place, though I was too depressed to realize it at the time.

The next day I said goodbye, got a ride to the border, and walked across. Once in Ecuador I found a bus to Machala. In an effort to avoid going over my time limit of 180 days for the year, I planned to enter illegally, and then return again to Peru three months later. I really had no idea how much longer I would last in Ecuador and thought three months would be enough time to let things settle so I could move toward something more sustainable.

We passed immigration and I thought I was safe.

A few minutes later the police stopped and boarded the bus to check everyone's papers. The single officer who boarded was not much older than me and his wide smile betrayed his visions of self-importance as he walked down the aisle scanning the passengers' faces. His skin was smooth and tan, and his hat was too big for his head, slipping down onto his forehead. The officer didn't question a single Ecuadorian and went straight to me, even though I was sitting toward the back. My passport would show that I illegally crossed the border, so I lied.

"*No lo tengo*—I don't have it."

"You don't have it? Where is it?"

Acting as innocent and ignorant as I could while purposefully stumbling over my Spanish, I told him it was in Quito. "I only visited the market at the border, but since I never went into Peru, I thought I wouldn't need my passport," I told him.

He seemed a little angry and began to raise his voice. "It's the law here that everyone must carry ID. I'm a policeman (pointing to *POLICIA* on his uniform, an action he would repeat throughout this interaction) and it's my job to arrest you. Where is your luggage?"

I reluctantly handed over my backpack. By now the whole bus was silent with their attention squarely focused on the scene he was creating. He quickly searched my bag but, to my great fortune, never found my passport. He repeated his dumb uniform touching and told me that he was going to arrest me, and that I might be deported. I knew that if I left the bus with him, the consequences would be dire, much worse than the officer realized. Upon any thorough examination it would have been abundantly clear what I was doing and would surely end in my arrest. A second deportation, far from the airport, would be much worse than my first experience. It was the worst case scenario most likely to land me in jail.

The cop and I were putting on a show for the rest of the bus. I was the quiet, innocent tourist and he was the arrogant prick picking on the foreigner. I politely protested his loud demands but to no avail. Then, the most beautiful thing happened. A middle-aged woman in the seat behind me broke the passengers' silence.

"Leave him alone! He didn't know, just leave him alone."

She opened the floodgates and soon there was a growing chorus of Ecuadorians coming to my aid. The police officer ignored the passengers and turned to me louder than ever, almost in a scream.

"You have to come with me now, NOW!"

I ignored him and let a dozen voices speak for me as they yelled back.

"Leave him alone! Leave him alone and get off our bus!"

The policeman ignored the people and turned to me. I sat silently and let the people do their work as everyone repeated themselves. I did not speak a word nor move a muscle after the first passenger rose to my defense. The only way I was leaving that bus was if I was carried off, and I had too many friends to allow that to happen. After a few last unanswered demands, the policeman turned around and walked off the bus, defeated. And we continued on.

The other passengers were strangers to me, but they put themselves in harm's way to help me. If they had not risen up in my support, I am not sure what I would have done. They had no idea how much they saved me with their courage and selflessness. It was a truly inspiring act and one that gave me hope in the world again. Underneath all the dead leaves, life still exists, tomorrow is still coming.

*

While traveling on the island of Hispaniola in 2009, I found myself on the other side of this scenario.

After visiting Haiti for a few days I boarded a van crossing back into the Dominican Republic. Because of the great economic disparity and a simmering animosity between the two Caribbean nations that share a common island, the border was tight and we were all forced to get out as soldiers searched for contraband. During the chaos of Dominican soldiers, Haitian police, and United Nations peacekeeping forces all walking around and speaking different languages to each other, a new passenger made his way into the van and took the seat directly in front of me. His head was shaved: sweat glistened on top of the tight dark skin stretched over his skull. His face was taut and his elbows stuck out as if his skin was a size too small for his body. His only luggage was a half-empty plastic bag he clutched tightly between his shaking fingers. I recognized it immediately; he was sneaking across the border.

At the first checkpoint I watched as he handed over a wad of small bills to a police officer. At the second checkpoint a burly officer poked into the van and, looking around, asked the skinny man in front of me for his passport. When he couldn't provide one, he asked him to step outside the van.

I read the name off the policeman's uniform. "Mr. Gomez, he only got on a mile or two down the road. Please, I'm in a hurry to get back to Santo Domingo [the Dominican capital]," I said in perfect Spanish. Surprised, he stared back at me inquisitively for a second before taking a step back.

"Make sure your friend brings his passport next time or there will be trouble."

From that point onward, at every checkpoint, each of the passengers, all of us strangers to this man, defended him and resisted any police trying to remove him. When we got to Santo Domingo, the skinny man stepped out of the van and disappeared into a sea of people. He made it.

Crossing Five

April 23, 2007

The Final Crossing

In the cold, pouring rain that was closing out the wet season, I ran through the dark streets of Latacunga and quickly found a bus to Machala. As the bus sped southward Lucía called me.

"I just wanted to see how you were," she said.

"I'm fine. Are you okay?" I asked.

"I'm fine."

Silence held the line and a wave of sadness washed over me as I imagined her on the other end, holding the phone against her ear, waiting for me to say something.

"Okay, well, I just wanted to see how you were. Goodnight," she said.

"Goodnight."

I held the phone in my hand, staring at her phone number, encased in the depression that had held me for too long. I was leaving, running home, running to New York, running as fast as I could. According to my passport I was in Peru, thus I had to return there in order to officially leave it and then enter Ecuador. Once I was again legal in Ecuador, I could buy a plane ticket and fly far, far away—fly back to New York.

I wanted my departure to be like ripping off a Band-Aid, hoping the sharp pain would be over sooner if I did it fast. I wanted to say my goodbyes in Latacunga and be on a plane that same day. I had built a new life for myself in Ecuador. I lost the woman I loved, I fought bitterly with my university when I thought it became a political tool, and I lost hope in a land that spit on me when I smiled at it. Still, I had developed a deep attachment to the place I once called home. I met a lot of great people and learned so much, so that despite all my heartache, part of me desperately wanted to stay and ride out the storm.

The bus to the border was uncomfortable and crowded. It allowed me almost no sleep until we reached Machala at 4:30 a.m. From there I awaited my final encounter with the border police. I considered getting off in Machala to wait a few hours in order to cross the border area in unsuspicious daylight, but decided to test my luck and continue on. I no longer cared about the consequences, I was simply going through the motions. I had stopped caring what could happen to me. I was indifferent, broken.

We never got stopped. The darkness was fading as I stepped off the bus in Huaquillas and I was immediately hounded by men working the border. I agreed to a taxi to Peruvian immigration. The driver was a thief and looked for ways to rip me off. When his numerous scams failed he simply demanded a much higher fare than we had agreed upon. I was in no mood and aggressively resisted.

"I won't give you anything else," I told him. When he refused to take the money from my hand I let the fare we had agreed upon fall to the ground. I turned my back and walked away.

"Come back here, you need to pay more, I'll be waiting for you," he said, following me toward immigration.

I ignored him and kept walking, determined to win this small victory. Then I watched as he joined two police officers in conversation. They slapped him on the back and called him by his first name; they were clearly all friends. That changed things.

I turned back, smiled and paid more than double what I should have. I wanted the *taxista* gone as fast as possible. The driver knew I was entering rather than leaving Peru, and if the police discovered that he had driven me from Ecuador and they checked my passport they would have realized I was manipulating my immigration status.

Though this particular *taxista* did not know it, I was in a vulnerable position. Anytime that I crossed I was vulnerable. The modern border has evolved in opposition to the needs and desires of humanity, consequently creating a vast international black market. Trafficking in human beings is the third largest criminal enterprise in the world, and anyone who crosses, with help or not, becomes easy prey for individuals with low morals. Illegals live in fear of the police and are unlikely to seek their help. This makes them easy targets and helps turn some crossers into sex slaves, and lets smugglers rape and kill with little consequence. Borders are full of people ready to profit off exploitation: a cabbie raising your fare; a money changer altering the exchange rate or passing false bills; an airline taking money from a bank account without authorization; or a police officer demanding a bribe in exchange for your freedom. Rather than making a given nation safer, quite the contrary has happened, and a powerful criminal element has risen.

Outside I took a *moto* back to the international bridge. The small, soft-spoken driver's friendly and honest demeanor seemed out of place at the border, but good people exist everywhere.

At immigration in Ecuador I waited on line while three men bribed the police in front of me. I wondered what their story was.

Epilogue

Ecuador, 2017

When I returned to Ecuador this year I landed at a new airport. Still, it felt odd walking down the corridor toward immigration. I had never been in this building before, but it was eerily familiar. At the top of the stairs, as I looked down upon immigration control below, I felt a pulse of nostalgia or fear—it was hard to tell which. I had to remind myself that that was a long time ago, in a different place.

My heart beat faster as I approached the immigration counter. I've spent the past decade traveling the world, yet crossing borders always makes me nervous. I've been through a hundred immigration counters and should know the procedures by now, but a kind of blankness sometimes takes over as I approach, especially in Ecuador.

I handed the officer the wrong form.

"Only passport." She smiled, struggling to speak English. "This Customs. There." She handed me back the form and pointed behind her.

"Okay. Thank you."

She smiled again.

She scanned my passport, typed at her keyboard then paused. She typed more, then stared at her screen as if unsure how to proceed. Her eyes crunched in confusion. She spoke in Spanish.

"You were deported in 2006?"

"Yes. But I've been back since."

"You were last here in 2015, correct?"

"Yes."

Her eyes darted between her screen and me. "There is an alert on your passport but I can't see why. The only thing I see is the deportation."

"But I've been back since without any problems."

"It looks like the alert is new, but I'm not sure why. I must inform my supervisor that you are at immigration. Wait here." She took my passport and walked away.

I stood at the empty desk, alone, staring forward and into Ecuador.

I didn't tell the officer, but the last time I was in the country, two years prior, I may have upset the government. I had come back to write an article for *The Guardian* about a new digital dollar that the country was planning to issue—a pet project of Correa, who had been an economist before he ran for president. I had worked closely with one of the heads of the Central Bank of Ecuador who was charged with creating the money. We spoke almost every day while I was researching and writing and he told me he communicated with Correa about the forthcoming article. They were excited that their project was getting international coverage. In the article, I quoted my source at the Central Bank of Ecuador and the official rationale for the project. I also gave room to an opposition. Correa had successfully consolidated an increasing amount of power in himself but the president was missing one important tool. Since the dollarization in 2000, when the country abandoned its native currency in favor of the U.S. dollar, Ecuador did not have the power to influence its economy by printing money. Many in the opposition saw the digital dollar as a way around this limitation and regarded the initiative as little more than another power grab. I left the country before the article was published and my contact stopped returning my emails. I also wrote another article, for a much smaller magazine, that outlined how Correa, once the candidate of the social movements, had crushed those same social movements once in power and did his best to destroy a free press.

The president was famous for clamping down on dissent, especially when it came from the press. In 2010, he called in the military to put down a protest by police, resulting in eight deaths. *El Universo* published a scathing editorial against the president and his violent reaction. In response, Correa personally sued the author of the editorial, the paper's owners and the paper itself. The president made room in his schedule to sit in court for the trial. It's doubtful that any judge who ruled against him would have kept his job. Correa won the case. The journalist and two others were sentenced to a minimum three years in jail and a fine that totaled more than $40 million—an astronomical figure for a personal settlement in Ecuador. The journalist went into hiding and was granted political asylum in the United States.

As I stood at the counter and the minutes dragged, I wondered what would happen. It had been half an hour since the officer left. Paranoia invaded my consciousness. *Was this because of what I wrote? Will they deport me again? Does this airport have holding cells?*

When the officer did come back she took out her cell phone and snapped a picture of the photo page of my passport. Then she took a photo of me and handed back my passport.

"Welcome to Ecuador," she said.

*

I've come to the start in order to finish. I came back to Ecuador to finish writing this book.

There is a disturbing parallel between 2005 and 2017 for me. I left the United States that first time because I felt disenfranchised. I was ashamed to be from a country that had elected a president with values I vehemently opposed. This year is much the same, though I have a better idea of where I belong now. For a few months each year I work in the press office of the most idealistic and international organization I know—the United Nations. The rest of the year I explore places different from where I grew up, attempting to understand through experience and funding those trips through freelance journalism.

This time, Ecuador is temporary. This time, I'll push back.

With nationalism on the rise once more and immigrants increasingly becoming the targets of ire in my native country, I have never been so motivated to tell this story and try to show a different perspective, a more nuanced reality.

During my first days back I stayed with Ana, who remains my best friend in Ecuador. She moved away from her husband and lives with her daughter and granddaughter. Karmina, the little girl I used to pick up and toss in the air, is now a mother, and Ana a grandmother at age thirty-six.

When I saw Ana's mother, *La Señora*, for the first time, she was carrying rose heads. She screamed, ripped the flowers in half, threw them at my face then laughed. "He's here!" she screamed. She then immediately made me sit down and eat food.

"And Lucía?" she asked.

"I don't know. We don't talk anymore." I hadn't thought about her in a long time. I hadn't seen her since 2009 when I briefly returned to Ecuador for the first time since I had fled it. *La Señora's* question took me back.

Nearly two years after I left her, Lucía and I met in a park in Salcedo, a town between Latacunga and Ambato, and bought ice cream. She had divorced and was working as an industrial psychologist at one of the nation's new mega-jails. For a while we both sat looking forward, not saying much. There was space between us in the middle of the bench as if we were strangers. After we finished our ice cream we walked around the park then sat down again to talk. Our bodies now closer. I smelled her perfume and noticed her brown eyes, somehow different than I remembered.

Lucía put her hand on my knee. It felt cold and heavy. "I'm sorry about everything," she said. "I really did love you."

Her voice was quiet, her eyes sad. She looked away. "You really did help me. I want you to know that."

After spending so much time doubting reality with her, I felt sure she was being honest. She seemed to be talking more to express rather than get any reaction from me. She had never seemed so mature, so self-aware.

"I loved you too."

She looked back at me and smiled. And I did too.

We hugged and walked away from each other for the last time.

*

After a week with Ana I found a new place to live at the northern edge of the city. Next door iron rebar rises out of cement columns and reaches toward the sky. There is a cement foundation beneath the columns but nothing more; the house was abandoned amid its construction. Across the street is a massive vacant lot of overgrown grass and weeds. Cows munch on the grass and feral dogs patrol the edges. In one lot, the owners built a wall around their property and then abandoned the project, so now their lot of weeds and grass is more exclusive than the rest. Behind my small house concrete boxes are stacked on top of each other on what would have been a two-story building. There are no windows or doors, just holes in the grey concrete.

This neighborhood was abandoned after Cotopaxi erupted in 2015. It is now considered a 'Risk Zone' and no new construction is allowed, though even if it were it's doubtful many would want to live here. My house is one of a handful that were completed before the construction freeze. The eruption, the first in over 100 years, was a surprise but was also minor—little more than a puff of steam and some ash. However, it signaled that the 'throat of fire' is likely gearing up for a major event, the kind that will probably destroy Latacunga. My current neighborhood, *Campo Verde*—Green Country, will be the first to go. It's located at the northern edge of Latacunga, facing Cotopaxi and on the banks of *Río Cutuchi*.

Inside the city center there are blue signs with arrows on nearly every street pointing toward 'Evacuation Routes.' Inside all the parks there are maps of the city and lists of neighborhoods that are considered risk zones. Large maps of the city have been printed out and taped to walls inside pharmacies and restaurants. The predicted path of mud flows—the flow that will be created when the ice cap melts and the flash flood mixes with ash and gravel to form a tidal wave of wet cement barreling down the valley carved by *Río Cutuchi*, the valley Latacunga is built in—is colored red. Almost the entire city is colored red.

The Pan-American highway, once just one lane in each direction, is now up to three. And another brand-new highway, sometimes as much as four lanes in each direction, has been built parallel to it. Surprisingly, this has not reduced traffic. Just as the government has taken out large loans, so have Ecuador's citizens. Personal debt, once rare here, has ballooned and much of that newfound, if illusionary, wealth has gone into automobiles. The new roads avoid population centers. The buses no longer give you a glimpse of each town as you roll through it and fewer vendors come onboard to sell their wares.

The beautifully chaotic market I saw that first day in Latacunga, *El Salto*, has been covered over and replaced by a three-story concrete structure where vendors must rent small stores from the government. A metal gate closes off each tiny box when the vendor goes home at night. It looks and feels like a strip mall. Since I arrived that first day in 2005 the city has moved away from the open-air markets that filled all the plazas and dominated commerce. Chain supermarkets have sprouted around the city. And just across the highway from *El Salto*, across one of the dozen new or expanded bridges the government has built over *Río Cutuchi*, is Latacunga's first mall. It looks exactly like all the malls I grew up with on Long Island.

I came here twelve years ago when the nation was on the cusp of dramatic change, and it seems I am witnessing the death of that era now. After a decade of growth, the economy, heavily dependent on exporting oil and now burdened by paying back a decade of debt, is contracting.

My perspective is also vastly different. Young and naïve, I idealized *la Revolución Ciudadana* at its birth. When it didn't meet my, probably always unrealistic, expectations I became bitter in my disappointment. For a while I think that bitterness made me swing too far in the other direction. I'd like to think that I've since found a balance between those two extremes, and while recognizing that some positive things have happened, I still oppose Correa and his government based on repressive policies directed toward the press and social movements, two areas of particular concern to me. Though, surely some of that bias of my personal experience of wild hope then crushing disappointment still exists and informs my view.

Rafael Correa, once one of the world's most popular presidents and still a darling of many in the U.S. left, is now hated as a dictator not just by me but also by nearly half the nation of Ecuador. In the ten years preceding Correa, Ecuador had seven presidents. The constitution stated that no president could serve consecutive terms, which are four years each, though most were overthrown long before that. Yet, Correa ruled the nation for over ten years—an impressive feat. He twice rewrote the constitution and dramatically shifted power toward the executive branch while also growing the government. When protests broke out after he announced he would allow indefinite reelection he compromised by having the change take effect after the 2017 election which he would sit out.

Lenín Moreno, the ruling party candidate and Correa's former vice president, won a narrow victory, 51% to 49%. However, some early exit polls showed a victory for the opposition candidate, Guillermo Lasso, which fueled claims of fraud.

Here in Latacunga, police broke up crowds with tear gas. In what was a dramatically close election, the government lost Latacunga in a landslide: 61% to 39%. Few people I know who voted for Lasso liked him; most were voting against the government. Latacunga, one of the nation's radical centers, had been one of Correa's strongest bases when his government began, but the city has slowly transformed into a center of resistance against his government.

Correa has been mostly successful in co-opting or crushing the social movements that elected him but UTC has become notable for being the only university in the nation that resisted co-option by *la Revolución Ciudadana* for Correa's entire term.

MPD, that small Marxist party that was the only recognized party to support Correa during his first campaign, has become his bitter rival and still holds onto power at UTC.

The election protests fizzled out after a week. The spirit of resistance, the idea that the people could overpower their own government when it stopped serving their interests, is gone. The irony is that Correa, the firebrand anti-American populist, has transformed Ecuador into a place that resembles my own nation more than anyone else ever has—from malls and consumerism to political apathy and fear.

When Ana and I visited the highway blockade north of Latacunga in 2006, the one that sparked a nationwide revolt and put Correa in the spotlight as a champion of the social movements, I had never felt so inspired. In that exact spot, the government has built a mega jail which now holds five thousand prisoners.

*

Borders are everywhere. They exist between nations, fortified with guns and walls, and they exist inside each of our own minds.

It doesn't have to be this way. The world has become globalized for products and it could be for people too. When we buy phones made in China and toys manufactured in Mexico, we don't question that products have freedom of movement. Why shouldn't the people who made those products be afforded the same freedom? We can still have borders and still have some restrictions but why shouldn't admission to migrants be the norm, and their exclusion the exception? Why shouldn't we all be born with freedom of movement as a universal human right, and only lose that right after committing a crime?

Borders are built on a fear of the unknown. Critics will argue that as we tear down walls nations will lose their identity, but real-world examples demonstrate that this is not true. Within the European Union, though travel is unrestricted, each nation maintains its unique identity. On an even smaller scale, within any major global city there are a multitude of unique culture hubs that exist within adjacent neighborhoods.

Economics are a different issue. The familiarity of home has a strong pull and small or moderate monetary advantage alone is unlikely to be enough to break that magnetism; although when the difference becomes great enough it may suffice. Tearing down walls built by governments would not erase economic inequality; but it might lessen the gap. That shouldn't be a fear though, it should be a hope.

It's worth restating that I was born with significant privilege; that I was only able to travel abroad so easily because I happen to have been born in the United States. At times, this was a sad chapter in my life, but it could have been much worse. For the most part they were my own decisions and actions that caused my struggle. How different would my story be if I was born in Latacunga rather than Long Island?

My life will be forever changed by my own deportation. Not because it scarred me, but because it opened my eyes to something that had been hidden in plain sight.

Graffiti in Latacunga.

With Ana and Karmina in the family flower shop.

With Angely and Diego.

Acknowledgements

This has been a long journey and I never would have made it on my own.

Throughout this project so many people in my life have done whatever they could to help. The final product would not be nearly as good, or perhaps have ever been finished, without their help. All the errors are mine, as I still have much to learn, but a lot of the credit for what does work must go to the many who have helped along the way.

Michael Milano read the first draft years ago and continued to give me feedback until the end. Amy Dean, Adam Maria, Rob Murray, Nicole LeBlanc, Ryan Sariego, Nicholas Sweeny, Brian Gillen and Christopher Clark also read drafts and provided valuable feedback. They helped turn my ramblings into something much easier to read with their excellent advice. Kendra Leavitt and Danielle LaRose were wonderful beta-readers. Cullen Thomas and Marie Carter are former writing teachers of mine who kept in touch and continued to lend support. Max Elbaum helped me step outside my personal and much more narrow view of nationalism. Matt Crosta helped with setting up a publishing company and Eduardo Palacio made the logo. Steve Kistner never tired of being an enthusiastic champion of me and this project.

So many more people encouraged me and motivated me to keep going. Often it was when I least expected it—and most needed it. Even when I thought I was done, Ryan Marie Samuel suggested she could help me make crisper photos when she saw the proof and then ended up proofing everything else.

Every person listed here volunteered their time and skills and that means a lot. In most books when you read the acknowledgements it's full of agents, publishers and other people who got paid to help. Not with this. Everyone pitched in not for a paycheck but because they believed in the project or in me, and I am so moved by that.

My family has consistently been there for me. From the beginning when I was a naïve kid rushing off into the unknown until the day of publication neared, through it all I had their unyielding support.

Finally, I must thank the people I met in Ecuador who welcomed me into their homes and into their lives. People like Ana, Diego, Angely, Fabiola, Kleaber and Hilda who appeared in these pages and so many more who did not. Ecuador has become a second home for me and I am forever grateful to have met so many wonderful people there who make me feel that way.

Please leave a review on Amazon, Goodreads or wherever you look for books ☺

For queries: contactillegalbook@gmail.com